60 SECOND RECHARGE

Work And Life Ma...

Alan Hargreaves
& Patrick Cook

Published by

Wilkinson Publishing Pty Ltd   ACN 006 042 173
Level 4, 2 Collins Street Melbourne, Vic 3000 Ph: 03 9654 5446
www.wilkinsonpublishing.com.au

National Library of Australia Cataloguing-in-Publication entry
Author: Hargreaves, Alan, author.
Title: 60 second recharge : work and life made simple / Alan Hargreaves & Patrick Cook.
ISBN: 9781922178060 (paperback)
Subjects: Industrial management.
          Success in business.
          Organizational effectiveness.
Other Authors/Contributors: Cook, Patrick, 1949- author.
Dewey Number: 658.4

Design: Alicia Freille (TangoMedia) & Michael Bannenberg
Printed in China.

Contents

Introduction

A few years ago I had just written a review of a bestselling management book. The content was a touch indulgent but there were a few good ideas in it. I decided to blog about management theory the following week.

It was the same week that Patrick Cook started illustrating the *Recharge* newsletter. Patrick is no stranger to commentary and publishing. He's had seven books published. He read the blog and filed the cartoon below.

It was an excellent reminder of what used to be called Rule 42: don't take yourself too seriously.

I had always noticed management advice was often just blather. There are some nuggets of wisdom hidden in the big words, but there's also a lot of hot air. Buzzwords like collaboration and innovation are usually just teamwork or product development re-constructed. Leadership advice seems more about celebrity CEOs than real leadership.

What's more, successful entrepreneurs regularly break the five or six "essential rules for startups". People find their own way, usually by taking the most sensible next action rather than following an MBA playbook.

Patrick's cartoons are sometimes quirky, sometimes incisive, and sometimes completely unrelated to what I am on about. But they always remind me that we can over-egg this management stuff.

They also remind me of another development: the older I get, the less I seem to know.

This wasn't how I was told it would be. I had thought I would age gracefully. Things I didn't understand were meant to gradually become clear. As it turns out, they haven't.

There's some history to this. I first noticed it when the stock market crashed in 1987. I don't really know why it did.

Of course I knew more then. I was a talented young stockbroker, based in Asia and advising important clients in London and New York. I knew stuff.

I told them why markets crashed. Hadn't they noticed the inverse yield curve that developed prior to everything going pear-shaped? I mean, what were they thinking?

Like most brokers, I had an explanation for why things happened. Not necessarily before the event, but definitely after it.

I was a millionaire when I went to sleep in Singapore on the night of Friday, 16th October 1987. By the following Monday night, my net worth was negative. By then I could tell you why but unfortunately it was a bit late.

There have been a lot of explanations for that crash. Wikipedia lists program trading, overvaluation, illiquidity and market psychology. Those same issues turned up again in the last few years. But if you look at each of those items, they are just normal things.

Program trading simply meant that when the slide picked up momentum, programs sold the market even more. That's what happens in a crash. There are more sellers than buyers. Lots more. Machines can panic too, just as they did in the flash crash in 2011, and just like people did in 1929. Overvaluation? Well duh. Markets had been humming for a few years before the crash. Most put on around 50% in the months just before. Of course stocks were overvalued. Same thing last time around, and probably any time. Illiquidity? Equal duh. What do you expect to happen to prices when you try to sell something no one wants to buy?

Market psychology? There's probably something in that. People freaked out.

What's the most likely explanation? Things just went up to much for too long and had to come back down. Assets markets are like that. Property. Stocks. Bonds. I don't really know, but it sounds about right.

Businesses are like that too. They have good times and bad times. Very few last forever. With the exception of General Electric, all the original stocks in the Dow Jones index have ceased to exist regardless of whether they followed the latest management fad or not.

With hindsight, I could probably tell you why they failed, but I doubt I could have told you before they did, or at least in time to do anything about it.

Today we are awash with management theory, yet very little of it provides a sound basis for forecasting success. In fact most research shows that forecasts and predictions by financial advisers, political analysts and social commentators are wrong most of the time.

Even worse, those that are most wrong tend to be those who think they are most right.

This is why we put together this book. We figured there must be a hole in the market for people who don't know anything. The intention is not to undermine popular management theory. It's just that sometimes you can do too much strategising and take too little action. Sometimes you just have to get on with it. Doing so doesn't have to be that complicated, or that hard.

Alt

Alan Hargreaves

1

Getting your work act together:
Three basic principles

#1 Simplify your personal management system

Do you know this internal dialogue?

In the meeting: *That's great info. I must look up that website before the next meeting.*

Next week: *Where did I put that URL? I know I wrote it down in the meeting. Where was it?*

The week after: *I'd better log on again and print off that download. What did I do with the password? I scribbled it on a post-it note. Where's that?*

Just prior to the next meeting: *What were the key points I took down from that website? I wrote them on a pad. Where's that pad?*

It might not have been a URL. It might have been someone's contact number, or his or her address. Or a maybe it was the outline of that absolutely brilliant idea I had for a presentation while I was waiting in the departure lounge. *It was so clear in my head after I had drawn all the circles and arrows. How did it work again?*

For me, those dialogues stopped in 1995, when someone made a simple suggestion. Prior to that I had tried things like palm pilots, scribbling in my diary, Dictaphones and various other electronic inventions which tried to solve the same problem. They always looked like a good idea in duty-free. I would later try Blackberries, iPhones and smart pens. But so far I have always ended up retreating to the simple suggestion of 1995.

WHAT WAS IT?

It was the *Plain Book*. I call it that because that's what it was. I bought it at the local newsagent. I am now on my 18th. The original was A4 in size. It had 168 ruled pages. There were no tabs or dates. The only pictures in there were the ones I doodled. It cost $1.45.

The only change I have made in almost two decades was to switch to a smaller format Moleskine. There were two reasons for that. Firstly, it fits into the small zip-up leather folder that holds my iPad. Secondly, although it is more expensive, it looks cooler - or so my Gen Y daughter tells me.

I will buy another one at the end of the year, but not before. That's important, because if I buy another one, I may start using it. Then I'll have two and the whole purpose will be defeated.

There are three things I can say about plain book #18.

- It will travel with me EVERYWHERE until it is full.
- I will put EVERYTHING in it. And, most importantly....
- Nothing, therefore, will be anywhere else.

Everything goes in there. Notes I take in meetings; chance items that I hear in passing; the Internal Rate of Return someone said was essential for the project to work; URLs; flight numbers; ideas for anything; how much pocket money I agreed to give my daughter and for how long (preferably signed by her and able to be drawn to her attention later); suggestions for my wife's birthday present(s); great diagrams for presentation slides. Even the odd business card gets stuck in there. As I said, everything.

The problem I have with all the alternatives is that there is always one extra step to make it work. Have you tried drawing miniature presentations on your Blackberry? Or sticking a post it note in your iPhone?

Don't get me wrong. I use an iPhone for diary planning and for communication. But it is just not one-step enough for me to capture EVERYTHING quickly and with a minimum of fuss. I need to navigate in an instant.

It is not because I am I digitally challenged or techno-phobic. I am open to any new idea.

I got all excited when I experimented with a Livescribe Smart Pen. This is an excellent product. It's like a Dictaphone on steroids.

Unfortunately, when I tried to use it as a replacement for my plain book, I ran into problems. The pages were perforated and started to tear and I lost a few. Sometimes the battery in the pen ran out. Other times I took the smart book with me but left the smart pen in the car.

The ability to download my notes onto my computer is a great feature, but I invariably didn't get around to it. It meant calling up the site and doing stuff. I am one of those people who never look beyond the first page of results on Google.

I love the product, but by the end of the month I had retreated to my plain book.

I once managed a complex business transaction stuck in a Middle East transit lounge. It was the middle of the night just about everywhere else. I was able to this because all the crucial information was in my plain book.

Not that long ago I won a legal argument on the back of notes I had taken during a negotiation several years before. They were easily referenced. I found them in Plain Book #6. It took less that a minute to locate the details because Plain Book #6 was among the seventeen books piled neatly in the corner of my office.

In a seminar just after my 60th birthday I was asked what was the single best idea I had encountered throughout my career when it came to personal organisation. For those of you hoping for a digital solution, or an inspired matrix, or a motivational quote, I am sorry to disappoint you.

The best single idea I got was to carry a single book with me at all times. Write everything in it. Never throw it away. And when it was full, keep it in a single pile with all the ones that came before it.

#2 Clean your desk

What does personal disorganisation feel like? For me it's as if I'm lost in a sea of clutter. There's no clear focus, no sense of priorities and the nagging doubt that I won't handle everything that's on my plate. That's what it feels like.

What does it look like? The desk is covered with stacks of stuff, supposedly in order. The in-tray is overflowing. There are piles of unread "must read" material behind me. On the screen there's a backlog of unanswered emails.

It happens. Often I am top of things for long periods of time, but business trips, holidays, or urgent projects, can invite chaos into my office. It's not just a matter of how bad it feels or looks. My productivity plunges. That's because I am no longer able to apply four basic management skills.

WHAT ARE THEY?

Focus: Managers have a lot on their plate and a limited amount of time. Piles of stuff just distract them from doing their job.

Delegation: Getting the right people to do the right job is the core of management, otherwise nothing gets done properly. Failure to delegate is a good way to lose your job or your business.

Action: if you don't have focus and you haven't delegated effectively, you won't have time to take action on the things that matter. And there are some things that do matter. Luckily there are not many, which means you can take some action on most of them fairly quickly.

Priorities: Some things are better left till later. They may be important, but they just aren't right now. You need to get rid of them.

WHAT DO I DO?

I clean my desk. I know, it sounds simple. But there are rules. They involve aggressively applying each of the four skills mentioned on the previous page. If you do it right, this process will give you a sense of peace you rarely feel at the office.

To get started, pick up the first piece of paper you see. It doesn't matter what it is. Just pick it up and don't put it down until you have done any of the four things that you can do with it.

MOSES AND THE ONE PLAIN COMMANDMENT

WHAT ARE THE FOUR THINGS?

Abandon it. Most of the stuff in your office requires no action. It just builds up over time. The same information is probably only a Google away. It's just a distraction and right now you need focus. Just bin it.

Manage it. Who is the best person to handle it? If it is not you, get the right person to do it. Get it off your desk and onto theirs. Don't flatter yourself that you can do everything well. You can't. Humility is central to good management.

Execute it. If you have to handle it, take the first step. Just don't do it all right now. Give it some momentum. Make the call, set up the meeting, or set time aside in your diary to work on it. End procrastination by taking the first step. Get it moving.

Note it. If it is something that might be important in the future, make a note of it and send it to file. If it's too small to file then it is probably the right size to stick in your plain book. Just get it out of your sight.

There are times when I have seen this take all day, yet it can be the most productive day of your life. At the end, there is focus. You have already started. People around you are doing what they are supposed to be doing. Even you. Action has been taken on key management issues. Priorities have become clear. Important stuff is filed. The rubbish bin is full. Your in-tray is empty. Your management skill set is back in working order.

This is a very simple process. Remember the acronym: **AMEN. Abandon, Manage, Execute and Note.** Hardly rocket science but extremely effective.

3 Do more by doing less

I have often fallen victim to the massive annual to do list. I clear my desk in late December. Then I create a whole new rod for my back with an impressive forecast of things I am going to achieve in the New Year.

There are two problems with this. One is obvious. The list is so long that I'm already tired by the end of the first month.

The second is with my mind. When I've finished the planning, I start thinking about the outcome – rather than just taking the first step and getting on with it.

There is a lot of ego in this. Once I have made a great plan, I want to skip to thinking about how great it will be when it is implemented. I go straight to the buzz of achieving it, indulge in that thought, and start milking the gratification before I have actually done anything.

Next, my passion starts to wane to the extent that I have already enjoyed the result in my mind. There is already less gratification to go for. It gets harder to stay engaged.

And of course, unlike reality, the outcome is always perfect in my head. That just makes bumps in the road even harder to climb over and I have found that there are always bumps.

These are all good ways to turn something exciting into a hard slog.

WHAT CAN YOU DO ABOUT IT?

Try something different. Instead of setting a list of goals, identify some key areas in which you want to achieve things. Two or three will do. Make them broad categories, not specific targets.

For each one, choose an activity that you could do in that area. It might be the first step you need to take, or maybe it's the third. Whatever it is, just get started on it. It doesn't matter that you don't feel prepared, or even ready to make a start. Just get going.

Great writers advise budding authors to get on and write the book. The point is that action creates action. The first draft might be fairly ordinary, but you can fix it later.

Acclaimed author, E L Doctorow put it this way: *"Writing a novel is like driving a car at night. You can only see as far as your headlights, but you can make the whole trip that way."* It works for business as well, not to mention life.

There's also another good thing about not knowing the ending. If you focus only on the outcome, you might miss the chance of doing something completely different – something that might be far superior to the result you planned.

So start by writing a chapter rather than a book. You will be surprised at how much you achieve.

There's nothing really new here. These actions, or in some cases, non-actions, are generic to any advice on getting things done.

1. Whatever you want to do, just work out the first step and take it.
2. Forget the outcome. When you've done the first step, work out if you want to take another one. If you do, take it.

2

Should you start a business? Living the dream vs a rod for your back?

Type "business plan" into your search engine and you'll find thousands of templates. People write lots of business plans. It's something you have to do if you are going to start a business. But before you do all that, there is one key question you have to answer: should I do this?

At a rough guess, probably two out of every three people I know who have started a business wish they hadn't. That's not because they failed. A lot do, but a lot don't. But many make very little money and a lot are barely sustainable.

Nor is it because they didn't have a good idea, or lacked commitment or energy. It is more that it just didn't turn out to be as wonderful as they thought. It's a little like having a best-ever holiday. If you go back to the same place two years later expecting the same, chances are you'll be disappointed.

You might be passionate about your idea for a product or a service, but that energy also has to translate into a passion about running the business that goes with the idea. Without that, you can find a lot of essential activity to be irksome. Stress around those tasks can erode the passion.

Dumb reasons for going into business

A recent US study found 75% of employed adults wanted to quit and become entrepreneurs. It's a good thing they all have jobs, because none of the six reasons they gave are good reasons to start your own business. They were:

- Set your own hours: you won't, the business will. And they are likely to be longer than your full time job.
- Spend more time with friends and family: your own business blurs boundaries between work and play. Business issues are more likely to intrude on family time rather than be left at the office. Don't go into it expecting more time for golf.
- Get away from office politics: yes, if you are a sole proprietor. But that often means isolation from ideas and a limited ability to grow. Successful businesses generally need more people, and different sorts of people too.
- Be your own boss: you'll be taking yourself with you. You'll still be dealing with people. If social skills are not your strong suit, you could still struggle.
- Avoid commuting time: that's good, because you will need more time.
- Make more money: on a per hour basis, that's often unlikely for at least a year or two, if ever.

These are not deal-breakers if you enjoy stress, would like to work harder and want to feel insecure about your income.

Yet there's a positive side to those three things: properly managed stress can be a source of energy; long hours don't matter if you love what you are doing; and generating real income can be a motivating challenge.

Nonetheless, you need to be realistic. The hard slog of day-to-day operations and managing people can turn a good business idea into a burden. Having a goal like "I don't want to work for someone else" is not enough. You will still be working for lots of people, like customers, employees, suppliers, distributors, shareholders, and franchisors, not to mention banks and the government. You would be wrong to think you will be getting away from challenging workplace relationships.

It is also rare to have a seriously unique idea. You may be quite excited about a great concept, and you may also be capable of executing it better than anyone else.

Nonetheless, a quick search of the web will usually find someone else who has tried something similar. You need to see whether it worked for them – and if not, why not, and if it did, whether it will also work for you.

If you think you are on to something that will work, stress test the idea. Try to stand back from the excitement of it all. Get scientific about how big the market actually is. Be realistic about what percentage of that market you can attract and why, whether it's a simple web-based idea, a new retail shop in a suburban location or a major new product initiative in the national marketplace.

None of this is meant to put you off. You just have to make a very sober evaluation of whether your project is a good idea for you. Whether you like it or not, you will have administrative responsibilities. In an age of seemingly endless compliance requirements, you will have to manage many things that seem to have nothing to do with your vision.

You will also need people management skills and actually enjoy using them. And that's before we have even talked about how much money you will need to get started and where you are going to get it.

IS IT FOR YOU?

Find some quiet time and sit down and think about the questions raised here. Put a mix of honesty and realism into your decision. It may well be that you have solutions to all these issues. If so, and if you are inspired to go ahead, that's fantastic. Whatever happens, it will be a great ride, one that has a chance of being hugely successful. Take that passion with you. There will be times when you'll need it.

3

Start your own think tank: getting better ideas than your own

Once a month I have dinner with four friends. We are an odd mix, and there is a 20-year span between the oldest and the youngest in the group. We have one thing in common: we are all interested in business and ideas.

Mostly we just shoot the breeze. But we always finish with one simple process. It has four steps and it doesn't take long:

- We each describe something that went right in the last week.
- Next, we go around and describe something that went wrong.
- Then we run through something we want to get right in the coming week.
- Lastly, we describe how we each see each other getting that thing right.

The results are astounding. I have never left without a new idea or a new perspective. It might be something out of left field, something I just haven't thought of. Or it might be something I already know but I am just not doing. Suddenly my options open up; my thinking is refreshed; I move onto a positive track. The following week is always more productive.

That's a passage from my earlier management book, *Recharge*. It's about working with others and letting thoughts have a free rein. Managing in isolation is a dangerous practice. You can end up in a hall of mirrors with only your own thinking to guide you. You get stuck in tunnel vision and miss opportunities.

Often there is a better outcome through one of the side doors that you don't notice. You need other people to point them out.

This is not about forming a team. You form teams to manage a project or produce a certain result.

A THINK TANK IS DIFFERENT

It is less constrained in both its membership and its outcomes. You don't need people who are essential to the task. Nor do you need a specific goal. What you do need are people who enjoy the challenge of change and are happy to think outside the square.

Try this experiment. Gather a small group of people. Draw them from any stakeholder group in your life or your business – colleagues, managers, friends, customers, suppliers. It doesn't matter what their background or status is. People above or below you can be equally helpful.

The only requirement is their preparedness to offer both their own input and to give air time to the input of others. That is, to come up with an array of diverse answers to challenging questions like "what could bring about the collapse of our business in the next two years?"

See how many disaster scenarios you can come up with in an hour. You will find it won't be confined to the obvious like "losing your biggest customer".

Some scenarios will be outrageous, but in amongst the irrelevant or frivolous will be some real pointers to weaknesses in your business – or your division, or product line, or market outlook – in areas where you hadn't thought to look.

The key thing about weaknesses is that they suggest opportunities.

Narrow down to a key issue you have highlighted. Make the agenda for the following week an examination of what opportunities that weakness offers. If there's a problem, examine the solution.

SUSTAINABLE INNOVATION

You will be surprised at how this simple process can generate genuinely creative strategies for any business. Informal think tanks are a source of innovative action.

As with any brainstorming activity, don't reject any ideas. Even if one suggestion is that the business should be sold immediately, explore it seriously. You may find reasons why that is not the case. But you also need to be open to the possibility that it may make sense. It would not be the first time that such a course turned out to be a great decision taken at exactly the right time.

4

Management theories: yours or theirs?

Has management advice actually made any progress? Doesn't seem so. Prominent business leaders, management gurus, and leading academics – all three have a history of failure.

It can happen anywhere. I worked in Singapore for three years during the 1980s. Each year someone was designated "Businessman of the Year". All three nominees suffered ignominious reversals before I had left, including gaol time.

Enron regularly won the "most innovative" award in many a business journal before its collapse. The CEO is still in prison.

Market position is no barrier to trouble. Fully 25% of the Fortune 500 made losses in 2009.

Nearly half the companies lauded in Jim Collins' landmark management tome, *Built to Last*, have struggled since the book was published. Some have not lasted at all. Twenty years later, Collins wrote another book called *How the Mighty Fall*.

"How to" books by prominent business leaders have a similar, patchy record.

Biographies fare slightly better, probably because they simply tell the story rather than distill history into grand principles.

Nonetheless, if you read the biographies or stories of Richard Branson, or Steve Jobs – and most certainly Mark Zuckerberg – you don't come away thinking that they had things like business plans or strategy maps. Basically they just got on with it. Some things worked; others didn't.

Timing and luck always play a part. That's what business risk is about. You can't eliminate it. You can only manage it. Results come from taking the appropriate action at the appropriate time – something common to Branson, Jobs or Zuckerberg, or just about all the successful entrepreneurs or CEOs that I come across.

Strategic plans have their uses, but it is important to keep them in perspective. The use-by date of strategic plans starts ticking the moment they are signed off. Success from that point on is up to management action.

Do all these theories help us?

Some are inspiring. Some bring an element of clarity to our thinking. But mimicry rarely offers a solution. That's because you are not in the same business, you don't face the same environment, and most importantly, you are you, not someone you read about.

What is common to the successful biographies (unsuccessful people rarely write them) is that the subjects found their own strengths and applied them, leaving other people to apply theirs.

WHAT ARE YOURS?

Many people are familiar with SWOT analysis, where they have analysed the strengths, weakness, opportunities and threats of a particular business or product. It's a simple organising matrix rather than a silver bullet, but it can get people

focused on their own environment rather than someone else's.

Try doing one on yourself. Get together with some trusted colleagues or friends and see what you can put in each quadrant. Everyone has some strength somewhere. Working with others will highlight yours. Others will often see skills in you that you can't, or capabilities that you have but you don't realise how powerful they are.

Like any good partners, they will probably also give you some clarity around your weaknesses. The process will also make clear what threats there are to you using your particular skill set.

The result will be a clearer view of what your opportunities are. They will be different to the ones seen by Branson et al. But they will be yours, and they'll be based on your strengths, not somebody else's.

Reading motivational management books has value. They can give you ideas and inspiration. But as Judy Garland, an entertainer famous for her authentic style, once said, *"You were born an original, don't die a copy."*

5

Financial literacy: knowing
what you know

Aligning intuition with business arithmetic

You've got a brilliant idea. You know intuitively that this will work. You stress test it, fine tune it and finally make an excellent presentation to the board. You are on a roll.

Then a director asks: "what's the NPV for this over five years?" Silence. You've got no idea what he's talking about. Your confidence slips and so does your momentum. It doesn't mean your great idea won't go ahead, but you've hit a bump in the road.

This is the problem with a lack of financial literacy. It won't necessarily hold you back. There are plenty of self-made people with no business education and the issue can often arise with success. You were a great salesmen and an even better marketing director but now you are running the whole shop. Whether you like it or not, at that level there are some things you are expected to know.

Entrepreneurs can struggle with this. Having built a successful company they now have to run it. Suddenly they are seeking mezzanine finance from a private equity firm and it's all MBA-speak.

There are two reasons to not fuss about this.

- Firstly, financial concepts are always common sense. They are invariably based on simple arithmetic and logic that anyone can understand. In many cases you already intuitively apply them.
- Secondly, you don't have to be an expert in working them out. Your success is

If Simon has three apples and Sue has five apples...

likely to be a function of powerful strengths you have in other areas. All you have to do is understand the concept.

Look at the example mentioned above: **NPV**. It stands for **Net Present Value**. I get asked about this a lot. It's a simple concept that makes common sense. All it does is put some numbers around whether your great idea will make a better return than some other great idea, including putting your money in the bank.

HERE'S A SHORT EXPLANATION

NPV builds on the time value of money. Let's say someone gives you an IOU that pays you $100,000 in 12 month's time. Imagine term deposits with your local bank are offering interest at 8%. In that case, your IOU is only worth about $92,500 today. That's because if you put that $92,500 on a 12-month term deposit at 8%, you'd end up with $100,000 anyway with no risk.

(If the numbers look too simple, it's because I've rounded them. Trust me, they are in the ballpark.)

The problem is, an IOU is not a term deposit. There's a risk you won't get paid – in my experience, often quite a big risk.

So the value today is probably even less. You might think the risk of non-payment is 15%, not 8%. So if you discount your $100,000 at 15%, right now in present time, it's only worth $87,000. That's its Present Value (PV).

NPV takes this simple concept a step further. The word "net" is just the financial word for what's left when you take out all the other costs and expenses. Use it a lot around financial people.

NPV works out the value of an investment when a number of years are involved. You discount the money your investment makes each year, just at we did in the above example. Then you add up those discounted values and see if it is more than the amount you invested in the project.

That number is the NPV. If it's positive, you have created value, if it's negative, you've destroyed value. You might get someone else to work it out but that's all it means.

Another example? Say your great idea requires an investment of $50,000 and will generate income of $15,000 a year. It's not free of risk, so let's imagine the relevant interest or discount rate is 10%. That means the $15,000 you generate in the first year is only worth around $13,636. The following year, it's only worth $12,396, and so on.

Let's say you think the idea is good for at least five years. If you add up the discounted income over five years, then deduct the $50,000 you invested in the first place, it leaves you with a surplus of $6,861, so it is a profitable initiative. Alternative investments might do better, but nonetheless, this one gets over the bar of generating a positive return and creating value.

Like a lot of business arithmetic, it comes down to risk and how you express it. You consider it all the time in business and you probably have an intuitive sense for it. While there are sophisticated ways of expressing it, you can boost your financial literacy just by starting to express risk in percentage terms.

With any project you are looking at, focus on what sort of risk rate you think should apply. If you want someone to fund the project, including you, that's the sort of question they are going to ask, with or without an MBA.

You can apply NPV to anything. Try working out what your business is worth and see what your profit is as a percentage. Is your new project going to generate a better return than that, or a worse one? It's common sense. Does it add value to your business or not? That's all the director wanted to know when he asked the question.

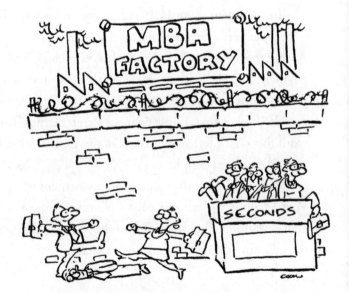

6

Why you should dabble

Add some risk to your career or business

A career and a business have a lot in common. Both are the focus of your working life; both largely determine your financial position; success in either can depend on the skills you bring to the party.

They also have another thing in common. People regularly question whether they can get more out of the cards they have been dealt.

Everyone seems to do it. Even entrepreneurs with sound businesses look suspiciously at more successful firms in alternative sectors wondering if that might have been a better idea; career individuals often plateau, querying whether they should have done something else. The trouble is, they never seem to know what "something else" should have been.

It's the common story of the school reunion: who would have thought so-and-so would hit a home run?

The reality is that home runs are often so-called Black Swans – the result of completely unpredictable events in which fortune smiled on those in the right place at the right time. Look around your reunion party and you'll find plenty of examples of the opposite. There's often a lot of serendipity in those success stories.

Could you, or should you, do anything about it?

HERE ARE TWO OPTIONS

Accept your reality, live in the present and just be. For low stress and a fuller life, it's probably the better option. You may even find that instead of you trying to drive things forward, a change of fortune will arrive of its own accord. You just have to get out of the way and give the universe a chance to deliver. It doesn't have to be a lazy option; it can be a contented one that is available for new ideas should they turn up.

The alternative isn't necessarily less spiritual. You current situation may be one that just doesn't allow you to make the contribution you are capable of. You are unfulfilled as a result. How can you examine this?

Take a close look at what you've got. If it's a business, can you do something else with it? If you have developed a sales pipeline to deliver your terrific product, look less at your product and more at your pipe. What else can you put in there? Amazon no longer just sells books.

If it's your career, are there tangential opportunities? If you have developed skills in a certain industry, look beyond that sector to where those same skills could take you. Real skills are often transferable with less fuss than you think.

Look for adjacent opportunities. What's happening nearest to you? If you are a supplier, can you develop your business as a customer? Or vice versa.

The same applies to careers. If you have built strong skills on the buy side, where can you contribute on the sell side? Stockbrokers become fund managers; technically literate designers morph into video producers; event organisers become campaign managers for large corporations.

Collaborate with people. Can the collective wisdom of your own team generate more and better ideas than the ones you can come up with? If you are an employee, talk to your management about where you can make a stronger contribution. Alternatively, ask colleagues or customers where else you could apply your strengths. Look for more ideas than just your own. Ask for help.

Nonetheless, use some caution. Don't bet the farm. Fresh ideas can have huge but unpredictable potential. Your existing situation may give you a stable platform from which you can dabble in more exotic enterprises, but contain your exposure to a manageable level.

Ditto for careers. Don't just quit the day job. Set aside a few hours each week to investigate where your strengths can take you in entirely unrelated fields.

It's simple actions that expand the realm of opportunities. Take a look at what you've got, in the environment you are in, with the people you know. Like a brainstorming session, be open to all suggestions. Don't disregard the apparently frivolous. If you think a certain idea won't work, look at why not. When you've looked at that, look at what would. Let some improbable events in the door.

7

Management confidence

The 6/24 Factor and the power of being you

Let's just say there are only 24 things that people are good at. There may be more, maybe less, but when I make a list of those things, I tend to run out of steam at around two dozen.

The list might include athleticism or empathy, mathematical competence, organisational skills, strategic thinking or the ability to concentrate, just to mention six.

Of those, I'm only good at two.

Overall in life, I probably do OK in a few more – in total, maybe five or six. Those are what drove my career. They generated most of the success I had along the way. Six out of 24. Twenty-five per cent. That's what it took.

WHEN DID I FAIL MOST?

When I spent time worrying about not being good at the other 18. Wondering what to do about that 75% was a personal hurdle every time I was promoted.

Perhaps that should be no surprise. Once you are put in a management position, you've got a lot of things to manage. As many as two dozen. The trouble is you

can't do all two-dozen things, just as you can't be 24 different people.

Promotion can be both uplifting and daunting. Suddenly you are running the team. On the one hand, you are excited and motivated, but on the other hand, fear can erode your confidence in meeting the challenge.

It's not confined to employees. I've seen the same emotions in entrepreneurs who have launched a successful business that they now have to manage. They are not sure they can take it to the next level.

WHAT CAN YOU DO ABOUT THIS?

Focus on the six things that got you there. Your strengths impact on the role you are given. It's often why you are in it. Job specifications are often designed with the candidate in mind. Whenever I promoted someone, I was often aware of his or her missing 18. I gave them the job because at that point in time, the role required one or more of their top six.

As a middle manager, the worst thing I ever did was chastise myself for my missing 18. Trying to do them was a waste of time. I wasn't good at them. Others were. Yet it took my team to tell me that. In one of our morning meetings, I proposed I undertake a new project. They simply told me not to. Politely, they said I wasn't good at that. They asked me to do what I did best instead.

So I did. In that brief moment of clarity I realised the key to management confidence is acceptance. Rather than get bogged down doing something you are not good at, find someone else with the right set of six and let them get on with it. It was exactly what my seniors had done when they promoted me.

Excellent management is not based on a fraudulent identity. There are all sorts of management styles. The best one for you is yours. It may be an administrative style, a marketing style or a strategic one. Don't change it just because you've got the corner office.

The 6/24 Factor is a rough rule, but it's a reminder of the things that will help you succeed.

Focusing on your missing 18 will hold you back. To build momentum and confidence, put 100% effort into your best six. They drive you and your team forward. When it comes to excellence in management, that's where great leaders make their most effective contribution. Focus on making yours.

8

To de-stress, de-clutter

Ever get that feeling you can't do it all?

You're right. You can't. When most of us build a "to do" list, it becomes an inventory of ideas that physically just can't be done in the time we give it.

I plan a month in advance. I write all my brilliant ideas on a white board and stand back at look at it. I think *"wouldn't that be a great result?"* If I stop there, it's not long before it's a rod for my back. There are just too many things on it.

Either consciously or sub-consciously, I know I can't do it all. The list clutters my mind. It creates distraction, which in turn leads to procrastination. The end result is inertia. No wonder I can't do it all.

That's why I take a second step. I discovered this when I made an estimate of how many hours it would take to complete each item. I added them up and came to 270 hours. That's nine hours a day, seven days a week, for every day of a 30-day month. Forget lunch, family, sport and pastimes. This was workaholism on a roll.

HERE'S ONE WAY OF SORTING THIS OUT

I made a conscious decision to work a sensible week. I took the simplest option: 40 hours. It didn't matter what days or what hours. It gave me a "time budget" of about 180 hours a month. I stripped out an estimated 25 hours for interruptions, leaving 155 hours for my list.

The next bit was the most important. I applied a simple priority scale to each item: one tick for something I wanted to do; another for something that would have a real impact. Some had both ticks; others one; some none.

I scrubbed off anything with no ticks. I was still over budget but down to 196 hours of things to do. Then I scrubbed off items with one tick, alternating between those that scored on motivation and those that scored on impact. The end result: 152.5 hours.

The real result? Clarity. I did not feel overwhelmed. I was motivated to get on with it. I had clear priorities and an uncluttered mind. My shoulders dropped as I felt some stress slip away into the ether.

There were other payoffs too. By choosing things I wanted to do, I implicitly chose the things I was good at. I did them quicker and better. There was less procrastination as a result. I wanted to get on with them.

For things with just one impact tick – like essential admin – I made an appointment with myself for the requisite number of hours. When the time came, I took the phone off the hook, shut down the email, closed the office door and did nothing else till it was done. If you want to feel good about admin, try doing it.

Another interesting thing sometimes occurs. Good stuff happens without me planning it at all. More spiritually advanced friends say this is because I have let go and given the universe a shot at running my life. This is the "less is more" view.

There might be something in that, and it was reinforced by a bigger surprise. I got more done than when the list was longer.

There are lots of books about getting it done. The reality is you can't do it all and it's counterproductive to try. For a simple recharge, be realistic. De-clutter your way to clarity. My children call it getting a life. I know they say that because these days I see more of them.

1. HIRE PEOPLE TO MAKE MONEY

2. SPEND MONEY

3.

But what if doing all that is just too complicated or too hard? Or when you are trying to counter silly personal management habits, like making burdensome resolutions.

HERE'S ANOTHER WAY OF SORTING IT OUT

It works well when your New Year resolve has got out of hand and you feel compelled to make a ridiculous number of undertakings. In empowerment-speak, it's also a "less is more" strategy. In old fashioned-speak, it's "quality, not quantity".

This is also a process that I find good to do with someone else. Friends are very useful. They know more about you than you think. In particular, they know where the line is between what you are good at and where you are kidding yourself.

What to eliminate? As I said earlier, most of us – or at least me – go best when we do what we *want* to do, plus a few things that we *have* to do, and let go all those other things we think we *should* do.

If I get that right, I get more done. More opportunities come my way, stress is lower, return on investment is higher and I don't procrastinate because it is easier to get on with something I want to do in the first place.

So, armed with an eraser and an honest friend, I approach the whiteboard. There are five steps:

• **Shorten the list of goals.** Be aggressive. What were the five most important ones? My friend's job was to keep asking, "Really, how important is it?" That eliminated the majority of the things on my list.

• **Avoid duplication.** Could any be combined into one? That got me down to four, and better quality ones at that.

• **Get realistic.** How much time would each one take? When we added that up, there simply would not be enough time to do all of them properly. I was still at four, but aware that something had to give.

- **Rank by impact.** Which ones would really make a difference? Down to three and time to do them properly.

- **Identify the doable.** Which ones did I really want to do? There were two.

What can I say about those two? Both were important. Each were sound and comprehensive. I have the time and resources to achieve both comfortably within a year, stress-free. Both make a difference to my life. They are good for my sense of achievement. I can't wait to get started on them.

THE HARD PART?

Letting go of all those things that my ego tells me I should be doing. There is a way to sort that out too. I work out the first action I have to take on one of my chosen two and take it. Suddenly I'm moving. Once I do that, I'm inching forward. Motivation picks up, momentum builds and those other things recede into the background. I'm on my way.

These are pretty simple processes. Both work for me. If you are already overburdened with excess resolutions for this year, they will work for you too. There are only five steps. You can do it with a friend, and yes, you can try it at home.

9

To feel better, feel worse

Handling negative situations

How hard is it to keep that sunny outlook going when you are surrounded by negative people?

For some reason, we feel we should be above this; that we can maintain our personal dignity despite the environment conspiring to press all our buttons.

CAN WE ACTUALLY ESCAPE IT?

I wonder. Many people learn to not react. That gets you part of the way. It also avoids escalation. In the words of my daughter, a closed mouth gathers no foot.

Not responding, however, doesn't always neutralise negative feelings. They just hang around below the surface taking the edge off your performance.

There's also the notion of "handing it over".

This is an excellent practice for the spiritually advanced. But for people in my less enlightened category, it's sometimes only a superficial fix. For a start, nothing has actually been processed. We have not experienced the feeling in full. We have simply packaged it for sending and sent it somewhere.

A quick handover can be closer to denial than learning, and certainly a long way from acceptance and closure. I've often "handed over" only to find I'm still stewing hours, maybe days, later.

DO NOT BOTTLE YOUR FEELINGS

DO NOT HAND OVER YOUR FEELINGS.

SO WHAT CAN WE DO?

Here's what works for me some of the time. It's not my idea. I'd like to say I got it from a guru I stumbled on when walking the Himalayas but the fact is I can't remember who it was. There was no white light and it's pretty straightforward.

Feeling angry about someone or something? Try sitting there and feeling really, really angry with that person or thing, full-bore, non-stop for twenty minutes. Do the opposite of denying it. Get right into it.

Ditto if feeling fear. Try feeling as scared as possible for long as possible. I've never been able to go the full twenty. The best I can do is about 10 minutes.

WHAT HAPPENS THEN?

The intensity of the feeling gradually abates. I'm not quite so angry or fearful. Sometimes there is even an inkling of generosity toward a person who has made me angry. Occasionally I catch a glimpse of a different perspective; maybe even a solution.

It's at that point that I can "hand it over". There's some closure because I haven't denied the emotions, I've actually processed them.

I've had great results from this in business, from handling difficult employees to managing tough negotiations. It is not always convenient to do it immediately but it's a handy exercise in a time-out. It also works at home. Even with teenagers.

It can also be hard to admit that you're angry. Or scared (especially if you're a bloke). But then again, you don't have to tell anyone. It probably helps if you do, but it's not essential.

I've made another interesting observation too: the more I do this, the less my emotions get triggered.

There are lots of suggestions on how to handle negative reactions. This is just one that works for me. It may work for you. The idea is simple. Instead of dismissing emotions, try feeling them.

10

How to maintain business passion

Your great idea and the stages of love

You have a brilliant idea. Your boss will love it and you can already see your career growing on the back of it.

Or maybe it's an inspired concept for a new start-up. It's the one that will launch your entrepreneurial dream.

This is love at first sight. You speak about it in those terms. It's an expression of you; an extension of yourself. This is the perfect mate that will manifest your real desires. Just like the ideal partner, it will help you create something special.

That's the first stage of love from any perspective, whether it's a person or an idea.

Evolutionary psychology says this is a crucial first step in aligning two people in a relationship – the matching of two humans, who together will propagate the species by creating a sustainable family. In business, that's you and your idea.

Much of this first stage is chemically induced. Adrenalin, dopamine and serotonin fuel the excitement. These are the natural drugs that lift our energy and give us passion.

Eventually though, like all drugs, they wear off. Initial enthusiasm is exactly that: initial. What happens next?

There are a few common developments. Some may get rejected, and possibly depressed. Some may not try again. Others just lose interest and move on to the next "new idea" – in relationships, that's the next "new girl" or "new boy". There are those, however, who take the original idea to the next stage.

It's this last option that is essential if the great idea is to become a reality. It is also the hard part. When the rapture is no longer driving the energy you need focus and commitment to build out the idea.

The love analogy still applies. The lover – you – has brought yourself together with the loved – the business idea or vision. There is a creative tension here. Once you start to build it, the idea will have a life of its own with its own needs. They won't always be aligned with yours. As in a relationship, you may have to do things you don't want to do to maintain the union. A bit of give and take is called for.

I regularly work with entrepreneurs who have created something brilliant but are frustrated by the challenge of managing it. Sometimes they have to share part of their idea and hire managers to do it.

HOW CAN YOU TAKE IT TO THE NEXT LEVEL?

Three things help any relationship work through stage two.

Realism: look to the positives of what you have created. Let go of unrealistic expectations and build on the strengths. Focus on the things you can control. Preoccupation with shortcomings will hold you back.

Authenticity: figure out your role. Where can you really contribute? It is most likely doing the things you imagined doing when you were first attracted to the idea. Don't lose sight of your original inspiration. That's a source of energy.

Collaborate: don't manage in isolation. Form a think tank; get a mentor; discuss issues collectively with colleagues and partners. It will generate positive energy and stress test ideas. It will also put into practice the notion that "all of us is smarter than one of us".

There's also the third stage of love. That's when the relationship between you and your idea has found a fulfilling modus operandi – one that is robust and sustainable. Like any successful relationship, it may not always be smooth sailing but it's able to weather a storm.

But let's not get ahead of ourselves. Implementation is the hard part of any strategy. It's the honesty and integrity that you put into stage two that lays down the platform on which the final stage rests. If your idea has legs, forget about the long-term outcome. Give stage two your best shot. That's what is going on now and it's the best chance you have of ever getting to stage three.

11

Networking vs A Network

What does networking actually mean?

The idea of networking can sometimes fell like social purgatory; like standing around at a cocktail party feeling like a bunny in the headlights. Everyone seems comfortable except you. That's understandable. There can be a bit of social fear around those events. We have all felt it at some time.

To overcome it, I was always told to ask questions. It seems to work. People are more interested in you if you are interested in them. If you listen to others rather than yourself, it effectively takes you off you. Sometimes it even helps you identify a real connection.

That last point is important. It highlights the distinction between *networking* and a having a *network*.

The former – *networking* – can often just be about collecting business cards and having lots of connections on LinkedIn. It's occasionally useful, but it's not essential. By and large, actual relationships trump virtual ones and mutual friendships generally outweigh having lots of acquaintances.

A *network* on the other hand, is something far more powerful. It's about connectedness that is genuinely uplifting. Honesty and authenticity are at its core.

HOW DO YOU GET ONE?

People often focus on industry events. They are useful but the problem with them is you narrow the range of people available to you. A good network is more about diversity of input than the coalescence of people in similar roles. It's not about sales. It's about linking up with people you genuinely relate to from a variety of different perspectives.

Research shows that networks can have a huge impact on success. Those studies don't talk about having loads of acquaintances. They stress quality, not quantity.

To hone quality, you need to keep it to a manageable number. Few of us have real network relationships with more than a dozen people – the ones you actually want to call, and where both of you are glad you did.

Those are people you really trust. Meaningful conversation comes when you can be completely vulnerable and open. You need to be able to have a dialogue with friends and advisers where everything can be on the table. People need to see the whole picture if they are to give you the advantage of a full assessment from their perspective.

When I look to my network for ideas and support, it's often when I am struggling. I need to be able to admit that and be open to help.

It also means leverage. Someone in your network will always know someone who can help with whatever it is you are trying to achieve. If people trust you, they are happy to recommend you to someone else they trust. Your 12 people know another 12. Even at the first degree of separation, that connects you to 144 people. That's why you don't need a huge network.

Another hint for cutting numbers comes from a study by Cross and Thomas quoted in *Harvard Business Review*. *"Roughly 90% of anxiety at work is created by 5% of one's network – the people who sap your strength."* They have no place in your network. Let them go.

Keep the ones that really matter. Include men and women. Have people from other industries, hobbies or sports. Solutions and strategies are more robust when derived by a variety of inputs.

Ignore status. You get as much from people junior to you as you do from those above. You need both. Some of the best learning and greatest opportunity come from teaching others.

For a real result, keep your network small and manageable; keep it diverse and give as much as you take. A genuine network is a two-way street of trusted relationships.

12

Taking action in uncertain times

Sometimes it's better just to make a decision

We learn the theory of momentum early. Sit on a bicycle when it's not moving and it falls over. Pedal a little and it stays upright. You don't have to go that fast to get some control. Once you are moving, you get some options. You can go straight ahead or change direction.

You can also go faster, but when you do, it gets riskier. If you have to make a sharp turn, it will be challenging at high speed, maybe even disastrous.

Neither extreme – taking no action or going too fast – is much help when nothing is clear. In times of uncertainty, to paraphrase Pink Floyd, there's no one to tell you when to run. Do nothing and you miss the starting gun. On the other hand, going too fast can build up momentum in the wrong direction.

Both can be expensive.

Does anyone remember Iridium? In 1998, it spent one billion dollars launching a global mobile phone system. At the time, it was visionary stuff. The company launched 66 satellites, putting them in geo-stationary orbit around the planet so you could use their phone anywhere.

Unfortunately, it was expensive to use, handsets were clunky and the signal was quirky. It was too much, too soon. The handphone revolution turned out to be far more earthly. Iridium filed for bankruptcy within a year. Mobile towers now dot the globe rather than the sky.

Kodak, on the other hand, missed the starting gun. The 120-year old company went into Chapter 11 Bankruptcy in 2012 having failed to spot the digital camera revolution. The theory of momentum says you can go too fast but can't stand still either.

Action creates action. You are more able to change direction when you are already moving, even if it means a U-turn. But what's the appropriate speed?

For a start, a lack of clarity is not grounds for a lack of process. You may not have the certainty on which to base a full strategy but you can have a clear management process for examining the options.

What are the interim steps you can take that move you in a clear direction? It may be the wrong one, but you at least learn the temperature by putting a toe in the water. If you don't go too fast, you won't go too far before you realise you are on the wrong track.

Keep your options open. Bill Gates kept the out-of-favour Windows project ticking over while Microsoft collaborated with IBM on the in-favour OS/2 platform. When the door closed for OS/2, it opened for Windows. We all know the rest.

You also need to acknowledge the cyclical nature of business. Hard times may not be good times to try to build your customer base, but they can be a good time to build their loyalty. If times are tough, what can you do to ensure they will be there with you when times improve?

Look for opportunities to do what you do best even better. This may not be a physical product. It may be qualities that are inherent in your firm or your team – innovation, great service, quality, brilliant logistics or even simple things like location or convenience. Use them to experiment in adjacent areas without betting the farm.

Lastly, keep working the scenarios. Role-play the opposition. Get your team to brainstorm what the competition might be doing, either to combat their strategy or to copy it.

Whatever you do, avoid inertia and take some action. Keep your bicycle upright; maintain some momentum. You will need it to steer through the uncertainty and onto a clearer path.

13

So you want to be an excellent manager?

Are the usual things holding you back?

What are the usual things? They relate to these personal questions: do I have what it takes? Can I lead? Is my strongest suit strong enough?

The answer to all three is yes. We often stumble over these questions but there is some upside to the hesitation. It means you are self-aware. If you don't stumble over them, you may not have the humility to survive as a manager, let alone take the steps to make you one in the first place.

START THE DAY WITH AN ACTION

There are millions of words written about management and leadership. Too often they focus on the style of celebrity CEOs or people who have enjoyed great success. Yet there is often little correlation between those styles and what's required in your immediate situation. Many successful managers or entrepreneurs acknowledge that much of their success came down to timing and luck. What they did may not work for you.

WHAT WILL WORK FOR YOU?

Here are five simple things you should do if you want to be a great manager. They are not difficult. You can put them into practice right away. They generate authentic leadership that works for you and they help those around you excel.

MICROMANAGE YOURSELF

Start the day with an action. We are saturated with advice to work "on" our business rather than "in" it. Yet nothing happens if one doesn't follow the other. Find something that will take 15 minutes or less and do it. Most effective people – in sport, business, community or life – have a starting routine. It's something that sets them up for the next event, and possibly for the whole day, because something has already been done and dusted.

People notice when you take action. Virtually everyone I have promoted was a self-starter. Start getting noticed now.

COLLABORATE

Start your own support group. Get together three or four like-minded colleagues or friends. Develop a mutually supportive brainstorming group. Thrash out new ideas with them. Take your problems to them and help them with theirs. It can be in the boardroom, or over coffee or dinner. Get excited about your issues. There is massive career leverage in this process.

Try to get input from people different to you. If you are an introvert, ask an extrovert to help you, and vice versa. Research shows that quieter people can get a lift out of loud ones. Equally, it shows that outgoing people find talking with introverts to be a safe place to explore lateral ideas. A little bit of vulnerability goes a long way.

BE YOURSELF

There will be people in your business environment who do some things much better than you. Celebrate them. Encourage them, so that you don't have to spend time on those things. Instead, look at the things you do really well. What are they?

THE HARDER YOU WORK THE LUCKIER I GET!

BE YOURSELF

If you do what you do well, and do it often, and continue to take it to the next level, people will notice. How can you make your strengths integral to the success of the business? How can the business leverage off you? This is essential to your success. If you spend too much time on things you don't do well, you will never get the time to shine.

Exceptional managers and leaders fully appreciate their strong suits, just as they fully appreciate the skill sets of others. There is great power in authenticity.

HELP OTHERS

At this point, you need to spend time forgetting about yourself. The best way to do that is help your team. Great bosses encourage others to excel. This is central to making it all work. Just as it is easier for you to be yourself rather than something you are not, people respond to getting help to do the things they are good at, or to be trained to develop a skill they have.

JUST PRETEND I'M NOT HERE

HELP OTHERS

This is what good people managers do. They worry less about their own stature and more about that of others. They know if they do that, their own stature will take care of itself. Helping your team climb a hill will put you nearer to the top yourself.

MARKET YOURSELF

Selling yourself is not about arrogant statements of personal ability. It is about proposing strategies that you know you can deliver. Ask this of your support group or your team: what is the best initiative I can take that will assist this business?

Take into account your strengths and those of the people around you. It might be a simple action you can take tomorrow, or it might be a major project that will have a long-term impact.

Regardless of its scale, it will be something that draws on your real qualities. It will have the backing of your team and it will be something on which you can take real action.

Don't hold back on this. Pick up the ball and run with it. Your strong suit will be strong enough, because that is what this process is based on. By taking action, you will be taking the lead. Doing so will answer the questions raised in the opening paragraph. Your actions will show yourself and others that you have what it takes.

14

To overtake competitors, overtake yourself

Why your personal best is better

Competitor analysis is a great way to assess where you stand in the marketplace. If you methodically work your way through the key strengths of those you compete against, it will soon become apparent where you do well and where you could be doing better. It's a useful process; one that should be ongoing, not just a one-off project.

But there's a danger here. If you focus only on what others are doing better than you, it is easy to lose sight of what you do well. It is an axiom in life that some

WRONG

people do some things better than you. Conversely, you do some things better than others.

In business it is no different. Competitive advantage comes from all sorts of sources. It might be location, time in the market, technology, training, key personalities or something special to them, or you.

Some of these things can be addressed. Some of them can't. If your competitor has a natural strength in an area where you are weak, you can waste a lot of resources trying to address it. Another axiom is this: it takes a lot more effort to make a half way decent impact on your weaknesses than it does to lift your strongest suit to an even higher level.

WHAT IS THE ALTERNATIVE?

Instead of undertaking a major project to address a perceived weakness, try just doing everything slightly better. For example, if your business deals directly with customers, ask your sales team or your counter staff to go the extra mile for just one customer tomorrow. Ask them to tell you what they did at the end of the day. Start a dialogue around it.

In any business, make it work internally too. Ask both team leaders and team members what they did for one of their colleagues today.

Lead from the front. If you want a work environment as good or better than the opposition, do the same thing for one of your staff tomorrow. Ask other managers to do the same. Write it down at the end of the day. Share the information. Then do something again the day after.

Start building a culture or doing something a little bit better each day. Build on your strengths. Ask people what is going right. Then ask them if they can do more of it tomorrow. You will start to build momentum in the areas where you and your people are naturally strongest.

It has long been understood in sports psychology that athletes perform better – and consistently better over longer periods of time – if they look to improving their personal best rather than focusing on the competition.

There is a natural advantage in this.

By focusing on your personal best, you are constantly looking at what you are doing well. That in itself is positive. What's more, you get encouragement and inspiration when you do it even better. Do this consistently and the marketplace will also start to notice.

Many successful businesses started this way. When Apple produced their first computer in a garage, they didn't copy anyone. They just made the best one they could make. Apple still does. The iPod didn't simply reinvent the Walkman. It moved laterally into an entirely new dimension.

You don't have to be a Jobs or a Wozniak to do this. It works for individuals, for managers, for small businesses and large corporations. Keep a keen eye on the competition, but don't get bogged down in worrying about their strengths. Work on your own. Develop a culture of doing what you do best, then doing it even better.

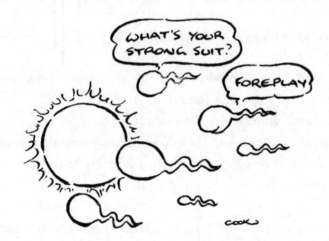

15

Treat colleagues like customers

Try this just for today

I once worked in a restaurant where the owner was totally focussed on customer service. The diner's experience had to be perfect.

Unfortunately, he was obsessive. It was like working for Hitler. If a waitress returned to the kitchen to refill a saltshaker, she would not be acknowledged for being on the case. Instead, she would be castigated for not having sorted it out before the diner arrived.

People hated working there. No one felt they were on the same team. Staff turnover was massive. The food was good but the business was a disaster. Disgruntled employees actively sabotaged operations. Customers who picked up on the negative culture didn't return.

Customer service has become a mantra, but if you want a balanced and successful business, you need to extend the idea of service beyond your customers.

WHAT ABOUT COLLEAGUE SERVICE?

What can you do to serve those you

EX-EMPLOYEE
★ OF THE ★
WEEK!

RECOGNISE OUTPUT

 DROP IN FOR LUNCH WITH YOUR TEAM

work with? There are common guidelines for boosting customer relations but you will build a far more cohesive business if you integrate those principles into all aspects of your business. Here are five well-understood elements of customer relations. I've amended them to apply to your colleagues.

Prioritise. Focus on developing a quality employee, not just a product

Provide quality. Make the work experience a positive experience; develop responsibility and let people take it

Communicate. Develop a two-way dialogue, not a one-way conversation. Ask questions. Listen to the answers.

Deliver. If you promise to do something, follow through. Let employees know that their needs also get some priority.

Check your attitude. Take a positive view of people's talents. Sometimes just being punctual is a skill. Acknowledge them.

WORK WITH SOMEONE

You can prompt this sort of cultural change by doing simple things. Identify someone you feel you can assist. Don't make it a massive task. As Mother Theresa said, "If you can't feed one hundred, feed one".

It doesn't have to be the best performer. It may be someone in whom you can see potential but who is currently underachieving. The critical question is: how you can serve that employee?

Schedule a session with them. This is not a performance appraisal. Communicate exactly what it is about

MONITOR JOB SATISFACTION

them that you really value. Acknowledge their contribution. If there is some small reward you can offer, do so.

Ask about their role and their personal development. Is there any improvement they would like to see in their position, skill set or level of responsibility? How could you support this? Serve them, just as you would a customer.

Maybe nothing will be apparent. Ask them to think about it and come back to you with any ideas. This is a small, first step in building trust and loyalty. You will be surprised at the result.

Corporations increasingly look on personal career planning as a staff service run by human resources departments. In many enterprises it needn't be that formal. What you have just done is take a first step in exactly the same process.

Ultimately, it is a step towards team development and the powerful leverage of serving others. By helping someone climb a hill, your will be nearer the top yourself.

Simple support initiatives often trump structured appraisal but in many large corporations, you will more likely be confronted with a formal assessment system, one that has to be undertaken regularly, sometimes as often as every quarter. This is more problematic.

Performance appraisal does not have a great record. Studies show it can curb performance rather than enhance it. Control groups free of such practices regularly outperform those subjected to it. There can be fear around it for the employee. The person charged with carrying it out is often untrained and finds it little more than a time-consuming irritation.

SO, SHOULD YOU DO IT?

If you feel any of the above, and have no training in it, the answer is probably no. Handled badly, it can work against relationships rather than enhance them. There is an unfortunate tendency to focus only on history and what is going wrong.

Then again, if you are in a management position, you may have no choice. If so, try taking an opposite approach. Focus on what's going right, rather than what's going wrong. Drop the word appraisal and take a mirror image of classic techniques.

Reverse the ingrained emotions you have around the process and focus on personal development rather than performance appraisal. Look at how to go forward.

Performance management expert, Robert Bacal, puts it this way. Appraisal programs fail because:

"...they're focusing on the wrong things. They focus on appraisal rather than planning. They focus on a one-way flow of words rather than dialogue. They focus on required forms rather than communication. They focus on blaming rather than solving problems. They focus on the past rather than the present or the future."

An appraisal meeting too often starts by focusing on a problem. No one in the process is going to feel particularly comfortable with this. The employee may be fearful or angry about it; the manager may feel discomfort in addressing it.

Start instead with something that is going right. No matter how small the example is, ask how they can build on that success in other areas. Search for an individual strength and start there. Everyone has one somewhere.

If there is a specific issue you want to address, focus on the solution. Ask not what the problem is, but what outcome would resolve it.

A solutions-focus generates positive thinking. A problem-focus breeds blame and negativity. Neither party could be expected to enjoy this experience, let alone produce a good outcome.

To work positively with your employees, listen to them. The best way to start listening is to ask questions. Don't stick to some pre-determined formula based on filling out a form. Start a dialogue. How can they take what is working and apply it to what is not? Go back to where this started. Imagine they were a customer and treat them accordingly.

16

Leadership in tough times

Handling a crisis

Taking off on a short flight twenty years ago, our plane lost part of its landing gear. There was a loud explosion; the aircraft listed violently. We knew something was wrong, although we didn't know what.

Within minutes, the pilot explained the next move. He would circle the airport while the debris on the tarmac was examined. Engineers with binoculars would assess the state of the undercarriage. He promised an update shortly.

The comfort of clarity

I can't stress how comforting it was to simply be told that he was on it. He was calm and he was initiating a process. We were no longer quite so much in the dark. His next broadcast was both good news and bad news: the starboard wheels had fallen off, but everything else was working.

The plan? We would continue to our destination. We were already airborne and we had to land somewhere. It might as well be where we were going.

The strategy? Emergency crews would be waiting for us. Cabin crew would make thorough preparations for an emergency landing. We would land on the nose wheel and the port undercarriage. He was trained in such a manoeuvre.

Our role? We ran through the safety instructions again. This time we listened. Some people asked for clarification; others diligently practised specific procedures. By the end of the flight I was a master at firing an emergency hatch.

I wouldn't rate it a stress-free flight but I am still here. Everyone did what they had to do. The landing was scary but ultimately successful. Maybe fortune had smiled on us as well.

Management in critical times

Former MIT Professor Edgar Schein says up to 90% of an organisation's culture is determined by the behavior of the leader. Specifically: what they attend to, how they react to critical incidents and what sort of role model they portray. In my eyes, the pilot on that flight scored 100% in maintaining a positive culture in critical circumstances.

Today, it often seems as if the wheels have fallen off the world economy. There are a lot of worried travellers around. Whole nations are close to bankruptcy. Business closures are up. Retail spending is down. Stock market volatility is extreme. Small bounces in optimism quickly stop at a lower top, and then head for a lower bottom.

WHAT CAN YOU DO?

Take a lead from our pilot.

If the situation is critical, acknowledge it: don't let the inertia of pessimism put you into the isolation ward. Assess the predicament rationally then communicate it clearly and precisely.

Make it clear you are taking action: many of your people will be worried. Let them know that you are on it.

Decide on your destination: don't hold back. Be positive and definite. Together you are going to get the business through this.

Look to your strengths: you are already airborne. What's working? If you have to land on only two out of three wheels, tell them that's what you'll do.

Get everyone onboard: let people know you will need their help. There is a role for every passenger. Collaborate to grow your options. Initiate action, no matter how small. Brainstorm ideas that let everyone participate. Taking action builds hope.

These simple steps will maintain morale and avoid inertia. That's what leaders do. Help your team to help you. Go out of your way to encourage action and give sincere thanks for results. Just as importantly, express authentic gratitude for enthusiasm.

Like all recessions or downturns, if you are in one now, remember they end too. If your business is struggling, step up to the plate and be the manager. Calm seas don't make good sailors. To paraphrase comedian, Jonathan Winters, if your ship is not coming in, swim out to meet it.

17

Want some change in your organisation?

Encourage joint responsibility

Collaboration may be the buzz word of the moment but "command and control" persists in management behaviour. It sort of goes with the territory. If you are in charge, you figure you have to lead from the front.

It's a hard model to break. Even if you practice that core management skill – effective delegation – you invariably just delegate the right to command and control to some other person.

You tell them what you want, give them the responsibility and the requisite power and let them get on with it. Individual responsibility, rather than shared responsibility, is often embedded in business culture. This kind of delegation perpetuates it.

Despite the plethora of management advice on "developing a collaborative culture", many change strategies are stillborn – great ideas but not a lot of traction.

TRY SOMETHING DIFFERENT

If you want something to change in your organisation, start with you. Rather than hold a two-day offsite to examine all the options, do something simple:

adjust your own delegation style.

If you normally put one person in charge of a project, put two on it instead. Tell them the problems; outline the goals; ask them to come up with a solution; set a date when you want to hear some answers and let them get on with it.

This is a simple first step toward collaboration. Real innovation often comes from middle managers rather than strategic plans issued from the top. Tap those resources. After all, it is the people in the middle ranks that tend to be focused on getting things done.

You may choose two people with similar skills, but be more adventurous. Experiment with a different mix. Want to improve cash flow? Put someone from sales together with someone from finance. Want faster delivery of your product? Put an operations manager together with a marketer.

I have seen this simple process gradually seep into firm-wide practices in businesses of any size. Improve customer service in a food outlet or restaurant? Put someone who serves at the counter together with a kitchen hand.

Don't be surprised to see this grow. The person from operations has a colleague with some good ideas. They bring them along too. So does the manager from accounts receivable. What's developing is teamwork, known today as a "culture of collaboration".

WHY DOES THIS WORK?

There are lots of reasons. Here's a few.

One is instinctive. Most species go better in groups than on their own. That's why we form communities. Leverage is another. We are all different. Collectively we are more likely to have the skill pool required to build solutions. Diversity helps. The broader the range of opinions, the greater the likelihood of an innovative idea. All of us have more knowledge than one of us. You are less likely to miss out on a good opportunity as a result.

WHAT'S ALSO GOOD ABOUT IT?

- People are both flattered and inspired to be asked for their ideas.
- It generates engagement (just to mention another buzz word).
- It can be practiced at any level in any business.
- It's simple and it's a start.

To get going, the only thing you have to do is clearly define the objective. People need to know exactly what is being asked. If the goal is properly framed, they will rise to the challenge of achieving it. By giving them shared responsibility for it, you add the seeds of teamwork and a platform for collaboration.

18

Why you need to collaborate

It's not just good for everyone else

Wherever your look these days, we are encouraged to form alliances. Collaboration is highly valued. Recently *Harvard Business Review* devoted an entire issue to it. Everyone, it seems, wants to work together.

Teamwork, as collaboration was once known, has always been a key to success. What has shifted is the growing openness to greater collaboration across traditional boundaries.

Diversity has been acknowledged – not for its political correctness but for the fact that cross-fertilisation of opinion and perspective leads to more robust decisions. It is the power of difference that is driving the trend.

This seems to be good for an organisation. It highlights adjacent opportunities, spurs innovation and engages employees. What's slowly dawning on people is that it is also good for you. It works at a personal level.

By you, I mean anyone who is leading or managing a team, or a bunch of collaborators if you like.

MANAGERS WORK WORST WHEN THEY LEAD IN ISOLATION

The big issues of the day, be they your own personal ones, or those of the business, are much more overwhelming when they only have your head to occupy. They take up a lot of space and crowd out the chances of finding a creative or productive way out of them.

As the saying goes, your own thinking often created them; it's unlikely that the same thinking will resolve them. Einstein said something like that, although probably more elegantly.

That's why you and your collaborators benefit from alternative, even contrary input. Big issues become a lot smaller when they share the space in a number of people's heads. There is also a chance that someone other than you will find a doorway leading out of a difficult situation, or into a better one.

THE POWER OF DIVERSITY

This natural advantage, coupled with diverse input, is one of the drivers behind the growth of peer-based management networks. Rather than expect creative management to arise magically from some irregular off-sites with like-minded people, the peer advisory model means regular contact with managers in a wider variety of industries.

The participants may have technically different issues, but underlying problems tend to resemble each other regardless of the industry. You are more likely to hear a creative solution listening to how someone handled a similar conundrum in a business entirely unrelated to your own.

It's a key reason why I advise anyone in a management position to draw on the wisdom of a purpose-built think tank. You can join an established one, or set up your own. Just make sure it is populated by a diverse group of people who can be open about their own experiences.

I say "open" because it needs to be a place where you feel safe enough to expose your own vulnerability. You'll get less out of it if you don't feel comfortable enough to speak your truth. Neither will the other members.

Try it.

The most constructive group I am involved in has five people with ages ranging from 35 to 60. Their businesses include privately owned firms employing two people through to publicly listed companies with hundreds. The results are stunning. I rarely leave without renewed vigor and enthusiasm, even in the most difficult of circumstances.

Collaboration works as a corporate strategy but also as a personal one. Set up an informal gathering of peers and share the issues you face. The impact of this small investment in time can be both reassuring and educational. Invest more and it can grow into a powerful source of creativity and inspiration. You'll go far further with the help of others than you will on your own.

19

Three steps to avoid micro-managing

Help people get on with it

Here's a quote from business professor, Henry Mintzberg: *"The manager does not leave the telephone, the meeting, or the email to get back to work. These contacts are the work."*

Most managers will relate to that. On the one hand, the flow of interruptions, requests and enquiries are a source of constant frustration. On the other hand, constant communication is at the center of successfully running any team or business.

What's the right perspective on this?

THE THIN LINE BETWEEN EFFECTIVE DELEGATION AND MICRO-MANAGEMENT

The art of delegation is assigning the right person to do the right job. That's the most effective way of making things happen, and making things happen is what the manager's job is. That's the first step.

Next, you need to make it very clear what you want done. There are lots of ways to do that but there is one simple formula that always works.

I learnt this as a young journalist when terse sub-editors would tear up my copy and tell me to re-write it. How, I would ask. Follow the formula, they would say. What's the formula? What, where, when, who? The idea was to produce a news article with a minimum of fuss that left the reader fully informed.

If you want a fully informed colleague – one who gets on with the job with a minimum of fuss – the same formula, re-ordered, will work for you.

Who: as I said in the first step, when the idea comes up, ask, *"Who is the right person to do this?"* Get people doing what they do best – choose someone who is good at what you want done.

Why: explain why this is needed. Tell them how its execution will contribute to the team goal. Tell them why they are the

DELEGATION: WRONG

best person to do it and why you trust them to deliver. Let them know you believe in them.

What: be very clear about exactly what's to be done. The end product will always be slightly different, but it can often be better than what you expected. Just be as precise as you can be about what you do expect. That means fewer interruptions to clarify what you meant. They will be able to make their own decisions.

When: give them a doable timeframe. Make it clear when it is due and why.

The last step is as important as the other two.

Let them get on with it.

It you are wondering where the line is between effective delegation and micromanagement, it's here. If you've got the first two steps right, give them the chance to do a great job.

USE YOUR OWN INITIATIVE!

MINES!

DELEGATION: RIGHT

They may come back and ask for more direction, but that's just asking you to do your job. They are looking for a decision. Help them make it but put the ball back in their court. Don't keep it in yours. That's just micromanaging. It will hold people back from excelling in their role. What's more, it will hold you back from excelling in yours.

20

Walking the talk

Had any courageous conversations lately?

Leadership is mostly about managing change. It is not always challenging. Sometimes it's a walk in the park. It is easy to lead from the front when you've got a following breeze.

It's when you run out of wind that it gets tough: your business slumps; office politics take a turn for the worse; there's a problem with your best client; your top sales team is getting poached; there are situations that can only be resolved by letting someone go.

THE PISSUP IN THE BREWERY IS CANCELLED.

These are normal business issues but sorting them out can mean changing the way things are done. Unfortunately, that also often means changing behaviour – either yours or someone else's.

Changing behaviour? Hmmm… Feel the shudder?

People naturally back off from these conversations. An open discussion about something like behaviour can be an uplifting experience, but it is also a dialogue that can run off the rails.

Having those conversations requires courage. There is fear around them. We are not sure how they will turn out. Confronting them means stepping up to the plate. What if it's a step too far?

It never seems to be the right time either. The danger

of course is it never will be – you'll never get around to it.

That kind of delay means the situation festers. Your management authority deteriorates and relationships fray at the edges. That makes it even harder to sort out. Inertia sets in.

Avoiding this vortex means taking action sooner rather than later. Staying on the front foot in difficult situations is not always our default position but it is important to remain on track. Here are some things that it helps to remember:

- Be a people pleaser, not a person pleaser. The fact is most people will respect you for addressing an issue. They may even be pleased when you do. They won't be if you don't.
- This is business, so commercial logic applies. Focus on what's best for the organisation – that is, everyone – not a particular individual. Stick to the commercial facts, not the individual emotions.
- Lacking confidence? That's good because your view might be wrong. Start a conversation that honestly states how you see things and ask others if they see it that way. Get more minds working on it than just yours. You will be surprised at the support you will get.
- Feeling vulnerable? This is also good. Real conversations happen when there is trust. People will trust you more if you are willing to expose your own vulnerability. They will feel safe about expressing their honest opinions in return. Your chance of a constructive dialogue will improve as a result.
- You are not the world's greatest leader yet. Your leadership style will always be a work in progress. Don't miss this chance to work on it.

All these things will help you exercise authentic leadership. Rather than having surface conversations that don't lead to any meaningful change, people will engage. You have a chance to encourage real shifts in behaviour.

IS THERE AN ISSUE YOU HAVE BEEN AVOIDING?

Try addressing it. Acknowledge that some messages are tough to receive, or tough to deliver, or both. Those conversations are part of responsible management at any level. Enter them knowing that that is your job. You are allowed to tell them that if it seems they've forgotten.

Stick to the facts. Explain how you see it. Make it clear it's your responsibility to find a solution. It doesn't have to be yours. It might turn out to be theirs. But either way, that's the goal.

Even if you don't enjoy it, a courageous conversation is something to feel positive about, not something to avoid. Not only will you be responsibly handling a management issue, you will be building your leadership skills. They will be even better the next time something comes up – which is also good because invariably, something will.

21

Letting people lead

Real change doesn't start in the corner office

Want to disempower someone? Just tell them exactly what to do, how to do it, and when to do it. Don't tell them why it needs to be done. Avoid any reference to the importance of their input, and never ask if they have any ideas on how it might be done differently.

Command and control had a good run through the industrial revolution. It didn't start running out of steam until the middle of last century. Even today it persists as a leadership option, often clothed in jargon about complexity and the need for simplicity. Got a problem? Don't worry; we'll sort it out with a new policy.

Yet some of the best innovation comes from the people at the coalface. Allowed to make their own decisions and get on with it, they can quickly come up with solutions to manage a pressing issue or solve a customer's problem.

MANAGEMENT-FREE MANAGEMENT

In the 1990s, the coach of the Australian women's hockey team, Ric Charlesworth, devolved leadership to the extent that the role of captain was virtually redundant. Criticised as leaderless, this team went on to win two World Cups and the Gold medal at both the Atlanta and Sydney Olympics. Not a bad result for anarchy.

THE MANAGEMENT PROOF FENCE

Charlesworth's tactic was not to eliminate leaders, but to acknowledge that everyone on the team was one. His definition of the team structure was "leaderful". As far as he was concerned, at critical moments each player is in charge of the game.

In business, leadership is the management fad du jour. Talkfests focus on building engagement and empowering employees, yet the biggest contributors to progress are rarely in the leadership group.

WHAT IF WE TURN THIS ON ITS HEAD?

Management professor, Gary Hamel, points to the unlikely example of Morningstar. They're the world's leading tomato processor. Yes, tomatoes.

Morningstar makes the mission the boss. Every employee draws up their own mission statement on how they can contribute to the company's goal.

What's more, they are given the power to take whatever action is appropriate to achieve their mission. They can hire, spend, and negotiate with colleagues.

The result? An engaged workplace characterised by lower costs, less politics, better decisions, greater initiative and increased flexibility. Pretty much the opposite of disempowerment.

THIS IS NOT JUST A PRIVATE SECTOR ISSUE

The disconnect between the leaders and the led is just as obvious in the public service, possibly even more so. Hemmed in by political correctness and compliance demands, bureaucrats regularly opt for *"one size fits all"*.

Yet recent experiments in education have shown that handing policy and decision-making back to schools invariably leads to better educational outcomes, even in the toughest school districts.

THE POWER OF MORE THAN ONE

Growing complexity does not demand the guidance of one wise leader. There is too much going on. What's required is engaged people who able to respond to shifts in the playing field at all levels and can handle issues as they arise.

What's refreshing about this is that it is not about how you can lead better from the front, with it's issues of isolation and associated risks. It's more about encouraging leadership amongst us all, be it on the hockey field, in the classroom or, for that matter, processing tomatoes.

What power can you devolve today?

22

Silent solutions

Try keeping quiet

Ever tried to manage a problem by not offering a solution? A lot of us automatically give advice. It's not just a Mars and Venus thing. Men and women both do it. Sometimes it is the right thing to do; sometimes it's not.

We are not all natural listeners. Some are, some aren't. For most of my life, I did not think listening was an action. I thought only the people talking were actually doing something. My wife has occasionally pointed out the error in this.

As it turns out, listeners are essential to a conversation. You can't have a dialogue without someone doing the listening part, at least some of the time. Communication is a 50:50 arrangement. For it to happen, two of you need to be involved.

Listening also gives you time for deliberation. That has value, no matter how little you put into it. You are more likely to get a clear view of a problem when you have heard opinions other than your own.

It also helps avoid the deadly sin of enabling. If you sort out a problem for someone without much of their input, they'll be less committed to the solution, and they will have missed the chance to work it out themselves.

Although guilty of it, most parents know this. So should managers.

How can we hold back from advice-giving?

Start by becoming a compulsive listener: ask questions. When someone comes into your office with a problem, ask this: what have you done about it so far? Get them talking about the issue.

If the answer is nothing, then keep at it. Next question: what have you thought you could do about it? Get the ideas out of their heads and onto the table.

Don't stop. If they have a thought, ask why it might or might not work. Ask what the obstacles are to putting this solution into practice.

If it seems like a good solution, ask them what is the next step they think they should take.

If it sounds right, ask them to get on with it. If they take ownership of the idea, they are far more likely to engage and perform. Building a team means empowering each member to exercise their strongest skills. Encourage them to do so.

It may be that the person who brought the issue to you is not the person to manage it. Maybe they will say they are not up to it. Then ask another question: who is the best person to handle this?

It is not always you. You may be the manager, but that's probably because you are incredibly good at half a dozen things out of the two dozen or so it takes to run a business efficiently.

That means that up to 75% of the time, someone else has the skills to manage the problem. Get them working on it. Get that right and you will have time to get on with doing what you do best.

If you want a team of independent self-starters – and what manager doesn't – try a strategy based on questions. It will often do more for the productivity of both yourself and your people than one based on answers.

23

Starting Up

Why budget forecasts are always wrong

How often do people produce a budget that turns out to be right?

I'm sure some people have, but I haven't. Even if the bottom line ended up roughly where I forecast it should be, it got there via an entirely different route to the way my spreadsheet got there.

Take breeding horses. That's something I do as a commercial hobby. It's not meant to make a lot of money. It's more of a lifestyle thing – but it's not meant to lose money either. It's a business and it's supposed to tick over. It sounds high risk but it is not necessarily so. My exposure to the racetrack is limited. I rarely race horses myself. I sell them to people who do.

I started my breeding program over a decade ago. It ticks over OK, but not in the way I planned. Yearling prices go up and down regardless of the quality of my pedigree planning. Prices have been entirely unpredictable. There is some correlation with the stock  market and the economy, but not so much that you can depend on it.

No one forecast the equine flu epidemic, which quarantined my broodmares and meant I couldn't breed anything that year.

Stallions go in and out of favour. It's a good year when I've got offspring from the popular ones; not so good the other way around. Horses are fickle when it comes to winning races when I want them to.

First we decide who does what?

And that's all before I have factored in the currency impact on overseas demand, paddock accidents and vet costs, plus the performance of past progeny – just to mention a few other variables.

This is all about business risk. You can't eliminate it. You can only manage it, and you can only make robust forecasts if you constantly stress test your assumptions accordingly.

The spreadsheet I put together 10 years ago makes embarrassing reading now. I still produce them today, but now I do it in triplicate: best, worst and most likely. Even then I usually test out what would happen if everything was 20 per cent lower.

Some years the best is the nearest; other years it's the worst. But over time, as I build in my experience and real data, there is a trend line that is getting close to the most likely. Not on it, but near it.

WHAT DOES ALL THAT TELL ME?

Probably the obvious. At the start-up stage, the chances of your forecasts being in the ball park are slim. There is just too much you haven't thought about and that you won't find out about until you are on the road.

WHAT CAN YOU DO ABOUT IT?

If you are looking at starting a business or a new project, examine every income and expense item and stress-test it for risk. This is a cash flow exercise, not a profit forecast. It's about survival. Make sure you are realistic about receiving money. Don't count invoices; count the money you expect to actually receive, and when. Forecast both late payers and non payers.

Look at seasonal shifts in revenue and costs. Check that you will have enough money at the right time. What if your best customer went broke? What if a supplier did? You might choose to ignore the things that are impossible to forecast – like fire, flood or earthquakes. But given the events of the last few years, maybe you should at least have a think about them.

The value of producing a budget is that it concentrates your attention on what the big variables are. These are the critical things you'll have to get right – or change your strategy.

Make a spreadsheet and fiddle around with it. You will soon see where your leverage is, and isn't. The goal is not to produce a result that exactly matches reality. It is to focus on the critical path you must take and what elements have the biggest impact on the outcome.

24

Retail therapy for management

Buying business

The business landscape is littered with disasters based on "expansion by acquisition". What seemed like a great idea to combine two small firms to make a much bigger one often leads to a smaller one, or to none at all.

Sometimes it's spectacular. America Online and Time Warner merged at the turn of the millennium. In 2003, they wrote down the value of their combined entity by US$99 billion. Small businesses don't get it right either. When the "dot. com" boom ended, literally thousands of small firms went bust after basing their strategy on rolling up small enterprises with rough synergies.

Why does this keep happening? One reason is that the excitement factor is very real. It's the born again business. Never mind that you are taking yourself with you. Suddenly you are growing exponentially in a dramatic transformation. Once these deals get momentum, groupthink favours a positive result. Everyone wants

it to happen. There's pressure to get the deal done. Issues like cultural fit or systems integration are barely scrutinised.

Then there's the numbers. Existing performance is rarely a guide; merged forecasts are built on risky assumptions about combined blue sky. Positive thinking generates unrealistic prices for the target business.

Add some leverage and a successful

outcome requires more than just a following breeze. One study found 70% of acquiring firms to be worth less one year after acquisition.

Yet you only have to look around to notice that many survivors are combined entities. Virtually every major bank has grown through acquisition. Most law firms or accounting practices I knew in my youth now go under the name of some merged entity. What are the drivers behind this growth model? There are three:

1. The risk can be lower – you can see if what you are acquiring is already working before you buy it.
2. Access to finance can be easier – if what you are buying is already working, banks and investors are more likely to provide the money to acquire it at a reasonable price.
3. Growth can be faster – rather than building a new business line or customer base, you just buy it.

Why do so many fail?
The reasons are pretty much the opposite:

1. Rather than focusing on what's already working, the merged forecasts are based on untested blue sky. That's always risky.
2. Most failures can be sheeted back to paying too much.
3. The need for speed overlooks the need for a cultural fit. Organic growth might be slower but it is more likely to keep a successful culture intact. Buying into a completely contrary culture is a recipe for a disaster.

Does that mean you should ignore this approach entirely?
Take a look in your own window.
Investigating an acquisition is a very rewarding way to review your own business strategy. Start the process by looking not at the target but at your own enterprise. What does it need? What does it do? How much can it afford? What, actually, do you think it is worth?

Take a 360-degree view of your existing business landscape. Consider your stakeholders. Is there is a business case for merging with, aligning with, or taking over, a supplier? Or a distributor? Look outside as well – and not just at your competitors. Add wild cards in unrelated businesses to get a lateral perspective on where you could take your business.

You may already have organic expansion plans in place, but as an exercise, spend an hour considering acquisition as a real possibility. Think about your space, your competitors and your future. The end result may be that you eliminate acquisition as an option, but your understanding of your own strategy will be deepened as a result.

25

The middle manager is not dead

It's more like re-birthing

It's fashionable to say it's over for middle managers. The theory goes that every-thing they did before either is, or will be, sorted out by new technology.

I don't know what business these people are talking about. But let's take an obvious candidate – Information Technology. Change in that industry is rapid, and technology is increasingly complex. But I have yet to find an IT company that isn't dependent on sound middle management to make sure they can reliably deliver their services.

What's more, IT is an industry fraught with over-optimism about its own ability. Ultimately based on the pure logic of binary code, IT solutions invariably make sense. The flowcharts flow and the algorithms are always the most convincing constructions of "if so, then….".

The problem is more "if so, when?" How often have you seen an IT project completed on time?

Like most of you, I have sat through some compelling technology presentations. But in my experience, IT proposals invariably over-promise and under-deliver. For realism, it's best to lower your expectations, prepare for significant cost over-runs and to

double the estimate of how long it will take. The issues with these projects are not to do with the great idea behind them; the problems lie in the execution.

Execution is what middle management does. It doesn't matter if you've got a brilliant C suite at the top and a brains trust at the bottom, good execution needs sound managers in the middle.

Middle management is not dying; it's being redefined. The skill set is changing, but it still requires skill. Someone has to make sure that something is happening. Try running any business where you don't have a strata of middle managers to ensure that strategy is turned into action.

This is not confined to IT. The management of any business is increasingly complex. Thanks to technology, we have dramatically more sophisticated monitoring systems. Executives are overwhelmed with information, from KPI analysis, market segmentation or ROI assessment through to complicated customer, staff or supplier ratings, just to mention a few.

While all these things are meant to help, they are also part of the problem. There is simply too much going on. To get through this, executives need to simplify their decision-making to a few key areas and delegate the rest.

The people they will delegate to are those with the capabilities that make up the new middle management skill sets – the people who run the help desks, the CRM systems or the teams of "people-facing" employees. They are the people who make things happen.

Middle management is a skill in itself. Anyone who is in senior management knows the value of these people. They themselves were usually one at some stage. It's great ground for career development. Running any team is an apprenticeship in leadership and collaboration.

Another reason commentators give for the demise of middle managers is that their function is being outsourced. Exactly who do they think are managing those outsourcing firms that are now doing payroll, procurement or logistics?

When MIT professor, Paul Osterman, did a thorough study of middle managers, not only did he find there were more of them, but they were more productive, more autonomous and actually got more pleasure out of their job.

That's good news. It means we haven't lost sight of the most basic ingredient in management success – someone has to take action; someone has to make it work. Yes, some careers stop at middle management, but according to Osterman's research, a lot of them are happy about it. They don't necessarily want more responsibility than they've already got. How refreshing it is to hear that some people simply like what they do.

Great leaders also emerge through the process. If you read the biographies of great business leaders, their resumes invariably include periods when the positions they held could only be described as middle management. Often that was  the platform from which they launched their move into corporate leadership.

To build a business that really delivers, love your middle managers. They are a crucial resource, a means of making things happen – and the likely source of the leaders who will eventually run your business. Be glad that they will know their stuff when they get there.

26

An environmental checkup for business

How's your economic eco-system?

The value of any business is based on two things: sustainability and growth.

Nobody wants to buy a business that cannot be sustained. A value placed on last year's performance makes no sense if the performance in the coming year isn't going to be just as good, or better.

If it's better – and everyone is sure about that – then that growth outlook will likely manifest in an even higher value.

It's not just business. Most things in this world are valued for their sustainability and their potential to grow. The human body is one. We value good health because it sustains life and allows us to various stages of life.

We value the environment on We may do so begrudgingly at times, acknowledge the basics of ecology: that underwrites the overall health of the inter-dependent. Mess with one bit and Sometimes for better; sometimes for worse.

Whether we like it or not, the comme. How business operates is subject to the same l science apply across the entire spectrum of ma.

WE ARE FULLY SUSTAINABLE UNLESS GRAVITY KICKS IN.

Your business does not operate in a vacuum. It depends on all sorts of stakeholders. Just think of the six basic ones: shareholders, managers, employees, suppliers, customers and the community. Together they make up the ecology of your business. Call them species if you like. They all depend on each other and have needs which have to be served. Often we focus only on serving the customers. Yet you can't expect your business eco-system to function optimally if you ignore the others. A truly functional business serves them all. In turn, that pays off in sustainability and growth. It is not a matter of altruism; it's a matter of ecology.

Look at each of the stakeholders. Shareholders won't be prepared to stump up funds to finance your business if their interests aren't acknowledged. Nor can you expect employee turnover to be minimised, or productivity to be maintained, if you serve employees badly.

Don't expect timely deliveries from suppliers if you constantly treat them as the bottom of the food chain. Managers can't manage without the support of the members of the board and the employees of the firm.

And the community? Well, that's where your customers come from. It's all a two-way street.

Getting that eco-system in balance is what makes a business hum. It's not some woolly theory. It's like spokes in a wheel. If one is broken, the wheel will wobble. You will have to peddle harder to keep moving and you probably won't go as fast. Ignoring this is like saying sustainability is not a sensible goal. Is there anyone out there who does not want a sustainable business?

So it pays to fix it.

For a quick check up, rate your firm's performance from one to 10 for each of the stakeholders. What can you do for the ones that score lowest? You might say, well, I'm the only shareholder so that doesn't matter. Wrong. What is the firm doing for you? Is it meeting your long-term goals in terms of value and returns? What, in turn, are you doing for it?

If you are a middle manager, what can you do for the manager you report to? If they go well, so will you. Can you work on a new service with a supplier in a way that helps both them and you – and deliver a better product to your customers and your community?

A successful business means interdependent stakeholders working together in a balanced eco-system. Ecology doesn't just apply to endangered species in nature. To avoid becoming one in business, try serving **all** the elements that make up the whole.

27

Your top customer is not always your best customer

Who's your most profitable account?

The most common ranking of customers is by percentage of sales. Most businesses have a few standouts. What makes them so?

Their sheer size is sometimes the reason: they are the biggest elephant in the room. But that's not always the case. Your particular product may suit them perfectly. Perhaps you are just dependable and they know you always deliver on time. Maybe the sales team on that account delivers a superior service. There can be longstanding special relationships with associated loyalties, or geographic reasons why you are the preferred supplier.

There are other, more subtle reasons as well. Maybe you do not monitor their receivables closely, and they know that you help their cash flow by allowing their account to age out to 120 days, when others are paying on time.

Whatever the reason, there is usually a cost associated with your success. Maybe it is free add-ons or complimentary backup services that make your product the perfect one. That costs money. The sales team may be your most expensive. Those cozy payment arrangements may be costing you in working capital and overdraft expenses.

To get a clearer picture, rank your customers on their net contribution to profitability. Where do they stand on a fully-costed basis?

There are sensible reasons to do this.

Firstly, you will get an accurate assessment of exactly whom your best customers really are.

Secondly, if it turns out your best customer *is* your best customer, it will highlight the sort of service profile, and cost profile, that generates a great customer. Can you extend this model to other market segments to create more "best" customers?

Thirdly, it will make clear the real relationship between sales and cash flow.

This last point is often key to getting your terms and conditions right. In an ideal world, the nearer you match the payment terms of your receivables with the

payment terms of your payables, the lower your working capital requirements – you either have a lower overdraft or more money in the bank.

Servicing a top customer often increases inventory costs because service can be a function of prompt delivery. The danger is simply stocking up to ensure delivery without monitoring what it is costing to hold that surplus stock.

Dealing with such "best customer" problems can be difficult. What are your options?

The obvious one is to set your payment terms as near as workable to the timing of your outgoings. But that can be a sensitive issue. Don't expect your sales teams to be your closest allies on this. They won't want to disturb their best relationship.

You can impact on that attitude by taking two actions. One, make it clear that their responsibility for your firm's welfare is as important as their responsibility to their customers. Two, to reinforce the first point, align their remuneration more closely to their customer's contribution to your profitability rather than simply on revenue.

Don't be embarrassed about having a thorough credit policy. Commercial terms are a fundamental pillar of good business. They make a statement about your professionalism and put a platform under negotiations. You may decide to make someone a preferred customer and to give him or her preferred terms. But just make sure you tell them they are getting special treatment. They'll most likely appreciate it and feel more inclined to use your services as a result.

There are also implications for risk management. If a "best" customer gets into financial trouble owing your six months of receivables, the impact can be harsh. It pays to keep them at a sensible level, even if it pays to offer them some concessions.

There are other options. They include staggered payments that bring in some cash up front. Demand management – that is, working with suppliers to match stock levels with cyclical shifts in your requirements – can shave inventory expenses. Service and maintenance add-ons lend themselves to "up-sizing" sales or building in steady retainer income.

Ranking your customers by their actual contribution not only concentrates your activities on optimising those relationships. It opens up strategies for building a stronger stable of "best" customers across your whole business.

When you look around your market, who else is out there that you could take from being an average customer to a premium client? What sort of servicing package is required to take them to the top level? There would be a price in doing so. A fully-costed appraisal will make it clear if it is one worth paying?

28

Cash Flow Management 101

Keeping it simple

When you look at a complicated cash flow statement in an annual report, it might look like accountants do anything but make it simple. Yet if you want to take some fast action when cash is tight, the basic structure of a cash flow statement makes a handy checklist.

It's made up of three very simple categories. Cash is either raised or spent in:
- operating activities
- investing activities
- financing activities

In plain English, those three things mean:
- what you do
- what you've got
- how you fund the first two

That's pretty much all there is to cash flow. Now you just have to manage it. For a simple health check on how well you are doing that, look at what you can do in each category.

OPERATING ACTIVITIES: WHAT YOU DO

All of the things in this first category are collectively called working capital. It's about the money (capital) that is working to actually produce things or provide the services that you sell.

First of all, you spend money to buy things to make things. It's effectively the cost of inputs essential to the production of your goods or services. If you run a

coffee shop, it's the cost of buying the coffee beans. If you make air conditioners it's the cost of the components. You have to pay for them. That means you have what accountants call payables.

Your cash flow management options are therefore probably obvious. Can you pay for them later? Can you pay less for them? Can you do deals with your suppliers to get any sort of favourable treatment?

Second, you sell the things you produce and receive money for them. That's receivables. Can you send your invoices sooner? Can you reduce the time lag to payment with an earlier due date?

The closer you go to matching the timing of payables with receivables, the less capital you need and the more cash you have available, or, alternatively, the less money you have to borrow.

Third, how much inventory are you holding? Stock ties up capital. Can you run a leaner business, ordering stock only when it's needed? Even accountants keep this simple. They call it Just-In-Time inventory management.

INVESTING ACTIVITIES: WHAT YOU'VE GOT

This is mainly about physical things like computers, machinery or premises. Do you need all the assets you've invested in? If your delivery van were under-utilised, would it be better to sell it and outsource to a delivery

service? Or has your business moved on, leaving capital invested in under-used or idle assets that you could sell?

There is a strong case for the business equivalent of a garage sale. When it comes to raising cash, strategies such as outsourcing, or selling your premises and leasing them back can make a lot of sense. Managing investing cash flow is about keeping your asset base de-cluttered.

FINANCING ACTIVITIES: HOW YOU FUND THE FIRST TWO

In most businesses, making all of the above happen requires some capital. A business doesn't go broke when it doesn't make a profit. It goes broke when it runs out of money. The better you do the above, the less money you will need to survive.

It's not surprising then, that what sort of capital you use and how you look after it is also a key part of cash flow management.

If you are funding your business with borrowings, including your overdraft, are you borrowing at the best rate? Can you slow down, or speed up, your repayment schedule? If you pay dividends, can you vary them or shift the intervals at which you pay them? What about a dividend reinvestment program? You don't need to be a listed company to issue shares. Can you borrow more cheaply from your shareholders, or yourself?

Cash flow strategy is not a static policy. Conditions in all three areas constantly shift. Make a habit of checking your performance in all of them. Tightly managed cash flow reduces your overall cost of capital because you don't need so much of it. It is also the cheapest source of money because it is about spending less rather than borrowing more. It's therefore the least expensive option for boosting returns and growing the value of your business.

HE PERFECTED THE CASH FLOW WITH NO REAL MONEY.

29

With or without you

Why branding matters

It's a big word, branding. People often think it only applies to big business. I recently read a blog claiming that branding is a luxury for small business. It's a common misconception.

Branding is about certainty and convenience. We buy branded goods because we know what we will get. That's what a brand does. It takes the uncertainty out of the decision to purchase.

Marketing 101 is getting the consumer to the point of purchase as easily as possible. You make it more convenient to get there by taking out the uncertainty.

The growth in Internet commerce can be sheeted back to the same notion. Point, click and pay. If it is not something that will land in your inbox in a few moments, it will turn up on your doorstep a few days later.

The price and the appeal of the product do matter. But those factors are a different part of the decision process. If your product does what the customer wants, the easier you make it for them to buy it, the more likely they will.

There are several plumbers in my immediate vicinity. I use one. He always returns my calls and he turns up on time. That's his brand. The others might be cheaper but I don't know anymore because I don't use them. I use my regular plumber because it's convenient to do so.

Branding doesn't mean you should rush out and sponsor a Formula One event. It means you should make your offering consistent at every level.

I never went to McDonald's for the hamburgers. I don't even like them. But when I had a car full of hungry kids and not much time and not a lot of change, it was the easiest decision because there was no uncertainty.

NAKED
FLOWERS
IN THEIR OWN
DIRT !!

I knew I could easily park. I knew exactly what food was on offer regardless of the location. It would be quick. The kids would like it even if I didn't. There was likely to be a playground, and the staff would be friendly. Ordering was simple. I even knew what the counter staff would say as I approached the register. The decision had absolutely nothing to do with hamburgers – although to be fair, I usually pilfered the children's fries. They were dependable.

Customer service begins with customer convenience. You brand your business by putting certainty into your product or service. That's more important than many other concerns that people have about branding.

Take quality. Not everyone wants it. For many generic products, cheap and reliable are the key characteristics. At the luxury end you often get little traction out of heavy discounting. High prices are part of the brand.

Nor is it about cute logos or catchy names. Build up the certainty first. Whatever your logo is, it will become known for the certainty it represents.

Another odd suggestion I occasionally hear is to not use your own name because it will narrow recognition of your product to people who know you. Try telling that to Henry Ford or Coco Chanel.

Or my plumber for that matter.

Certainty is also the basis of goodwill. That has value. If you can write a manual so that every aspect of your business is run consistently, it becomes easy to replicate in a new outlet in a different location or a franchise.

That doesn't only make your product easy to sell. It also makes your business easier to sell.

You may want to run your business forever, but you are mortal. When it comes time to exit, it will be a much more prosperous transaction if the firm can carry on independently. The ultimate test of a successfully branded business is what it is worth in the market, with or without you.

30

eMarketing and money

What do you expect for free?

The only thing free about the Internet is the method of delivery. Everything else costs – be it your online connection, or the free downloads you put up to encourage engagement, or the time you put into making it happen. None of that is free.

That's a good thing. It means that commercial principles still apply. It means that anyone who understands how to run a business can probably make the internet work for them. These are people who understand "returns".

With any marketing campaign, nobody knows if it worked until the results are in. That's why monitoring return on investment (ROI) is so important. It lets you know whether your investment is creating value or destroying it.

Most writing about ROI in social media is blather. It might be about "engagement", but if you haven't worked that out in the first five minutes, you need to go back to marketing 101.

ALL MARKETING IS ABOUT ENGAGEMENT

Here's a theoretical example. Think of Google Adwords, or the Facebook equivalent, as a letterbox drop for, say, a local coffee shop.

You design a flyer to attract more customers. You target a community, probably your local postcode.

You focus on customer service. You ensure the experience of transacting at your coffee shop is a positive one. You offer them a loyalty card for their trouble. If they buy 10 cups, they'll get one free.

If that all goes right, you have just bought a new customer. You've engaged them in your community. If they responded to the campaign and became loyal customers, they'll buy 10 cups of coffee and you'll give them one for free.

What did it cost you? The fact that you have "bought" your customer means you can work out your ROI. The cost of the flyer, its delivery, and the free cups of coffee add up to your investment.

For the return to be positive it has to jump just one hurdle. It has to cost less than the increase in revenue. No surprises there.

So how much money have you got available to spend on buying a new customer? That's a matter of working out your variable profit margin and it's not that difficult.

A SIMPLE EXAMPLE

First of all, ignore all your fixed costs. After all, they're fixed. In the earlier example, one more cup of coffee won't affect them. However, the amount you incur in milk and coffee beans will affect your variable costs.

Say you sell a cappuccino – or any product, online or in the mall – for $4 and making an extra one costs $2. That's your variable cost. Your variable profit margin (VPM) is the price minus variable cost, so it's $2.

In our earlier example, a "bought" customer may buy up to 10 cups, via coupon and loyalty card. At $2 VPM per cup, that's generates $20.

That's how much money you've got available to buy each new customer. Spend more than that on the campaign and your ROI is negative. Spend less, it's positive.

Spend exactly that amount and it's a breakeven exercise.

So the formula for monitoring ROI is pretty simple:

ROI = VPM X Additional Cups Sold – Cost of Campaign.

In our example, say the campaign generates 50 new customers and costs $800, including the free coffees. Then,

ROI = $20 X 50 - $800 = $100.

So you've made $1000 in sales and you've spent $800. Your profit is $200. In percentage terms that's an ROI of 25%.

Online sales are no different.

This is basic common sense. It doesn't change just because you use the net. The number you have to work out is how much money you have available to buy new customers – how much VPM they bring in.

Work that out and you now know what budget you've got available to spend on creating an online community, running a click campaign, producing free downloads, making a video, providing discounts for online purchases or generating new members for your site.

Nothing has changed because it's web-based, except that you won't be paying the post office to deliver the message. That'll be free. It will still be up to you to keep the customer, but that's about maintaining your community, not growing it.

Social media and internet marketing campaigns are exciting, but they destroy value if they don't produce positive results. Hits on the site are one thing; money in the bank is another.

This is not about sending the fun police into the exciting social media environment. It's just applying basic business principles to make sure it works.

People who make money online use business principles – either taught or intuitive – to create value. Try working out the actual return on your online costs. What investment do you have to make to build your tribe and what return do you get from it?

31

Climbing the wall of worry

Time to get off?

Because I spent over 35 years in financial markets, people often ask me about stock markets. What can I tell you?

Here's the truth: I have absolutely no idea where markets will end up this year. Or next.

I can give you some probabilities. I can name some stocks that might *outperform.* I could make some reasonably reliable dividend forecasts. I can probably identify some stocks that are undervalued, *relative to the market.* But as to the thing that ultimately drives absolute value – that is, the market – I have no idea.

That's because I have no idea about something like sovereign debt. That's up to non-forecastable things, like politicians. I don't really know whether one, many or any country will actually default in the next few years. I don't even know what will happen if they do. Maybe stocks will go up on the resultant clarity. The bottom of the curve for Latin America dates from Argentina's default. Things got better shortly after. Nor do I know if property in China will collapse or land softly. Or if Iran will both produce and explode a nuclear bomb. Looking back on the "fiscal cliff", we might all be better off it the US had gone over it. I don't know.

Welcome to the wall of worry.

At a health retreat last year, I was on one of those revolving climbing walls.

If you've never been on one, they are like a vertical conveyor belt. You just keep climbing, even though you are never more than a few feet off the floor. You do, however, sweat a lot. Or at least I did.

Nonetheless, you do have a choice. You can jump off and just watch the wall go by, or get back on and start sweating. You can do the same with markets.

At any point in time, is the cup half-full, or half-empty? If you look at the statistics since the sub-prime crisis started in 2007, you find that job losses bottomed at the 18 months mark. Job creation then picked up and continued non-stop for the next four years. Share prices in the US and many other markets also rallied for four years, almost in a straight line. This may have been the Great Recession but it was also followed by one of the great bull markets of our time.

Unfortunately few people noticed. At the time, we were on a fairly steep section of the wall of worry. It was clear to everyone that the sun does in fact set, but no one seemed to be watching as it rose.

It's not the first time this has happened. Since World War II, there have been 10 significant downturns in the United States. That's one every five or six years. Statistics are roughly similar for most economies.

While we don't know when the next downturn is coming, we can say some things about recessions with relative certainty:

- There are lots of them.
- They start and they end.
- They differ in length and depth but they all have a similar shape. Things go down, then they go up.
- If you are 35 now, expect another half a dozen before you retire. The business cycle is not dead. How you surf these waves will have a lot to do with your success.

WHAT'S THE CLIMBING STRATEGY?

In business it means stepping off the wall of worry and getting on with the things you are good at, like: maintaining excellent customer relationships, continuing to develop a great product, keeping your workforce engaged and delivering optimum solutions in the marketplace. That's what keeps the worth of your business – listed or unlisted – at optimal value in current conditions.

Unlike macroeconomics or politics, these are things you can influence. If times are tight, it is you who is in charge of cash flow management and internal operations. You can do something about that. While the focus may be on sales, you can work on your good relationships – with both your best customers and your best employees. Who will be with you all the way through? They will be a key part of your recovery strategy.

If market conditions improve, so will the value of your business. Given my extensive experience in financial markets, I have no idea when that will be. But if you manage those things to the best of your ability, you will probably be around to find out.

32

More on cash flow

From survival to value

Here are four simple financial objectives common to any business:

- Generate more cash.
- Cut interest costs.
- Reduce debt.
- Boost value.

Product and marketing strategies address these objectives at the revenue and expense lines. But for any company, be it highly successful or struggling, a focus on cash flow can also aggressively optimise all four targets.

The fact is boring stuff like cash flow management boosts your wealth. Every dollar you create or save is worth more than a dollar.

Before you switch off, look at this real example drawn from a client's experience.

He runs a successful business. Nonetheless, he had in excess of $100,000 in outstanding debtors stretching out past 120 days. He is a positive person and he is not particularly fussed by this abuse of his terms and conditions. His view is: it's probably a

I BALANCED THE COST OF PURSUING MONEY OWED...

AGAINST THE COST OF TWO LARGE MEN CALLED VINNIE AND TAUFA.

hassle to fix and I can afford it.

The reality however is this: it's not that hard to fix and the return on doing so is worth the trouble.

Getting debtors and payables into better alignment is good management. It may not be exciting, but it produces real returns at little or no cost.

This is what we did. Over a couple of hours we reviewed his payment terms and conditions. We aligned them with industry standards, ranked his client base in three categories, giving the best clients the best terms and offering standard ones

to the others. A letter was sent out explaining the new policy, adding that accounts over 30 days would be charged interest at a rate equal to the firm's overdraft rate.

Really recalcitrant payers (many way out over 120 days) were offered the opportunity to clear the outstanding for fifty cents in the dollar. After that, a deposit would be required prior to supply. Those not prepared to take up that offer were informed their account would be referred to a collection agency.

Tough approach? Some bad debtors ceased to be clients, but that underlined this old saying: if you lent someone $50 and never saw them again, it was probably worth it.

Most clients acknowledged the policy was both professional and fair. Rather than harm the firm's reputation, it enhanced it. The image in the marketplace was that this was a well-run ship.

The results? Not perfect, but three months later, no account was more than 60 days outstanding. His overall cash position improved by more than $90,000 and the firm's overdraft was reduced. Even the collection agency raised a few thousand. Interest charges fell by $796 per month, saving $9308 per year, which fell straight through to the bottom line. Profit therefore rose by the same amount. So three of the four objectives were easily met.

What about the fourth?

It's about turning a dollar into more than a dollar. The value became clear when someone offered to buy the business. The price was equal to 5 times his profit, which was now $9308 higher. In other words, the value of his business rose by five times $9308, or $45,000. Not bad for a morning's work.

Every dollar your save or earn in business is worth more than a dollar. Businesses generally sell for a multiple of their earnings. That multiple may be low, but is invariably more than one and it can stretch out to a double-digit number for sustainable businesses with growth potential in favoured sectors.

If you are wondering whether having tighter cash management is worth the trouble, don't just see it in terms of the cash it will bring in. It will do more than that. It will enhance the sustainability of the business, lift its professional standing, and most importantly, boost its value by a much greater quantum than just the amount you save.

33

Five hurdles start ups need to clear

Is your idea ready to roll?

They say passion is the key to starting up a successful business. There is probably something to that, and it does sound good, but in my experience I would have to put things like commitment and hard work up there as well – in many cases ahead of passion.

It is unfortunate but true that another element is also essential: cash. You may have some of your own but often it is not enough. You need to get it from someone else.

Finding funding for your great idea is always tough – even more so when financial conditions are uncertain. The market for startup capital can be squeezed at both ends.

On one hand, soft valuations put exit sales into limbo. On the other hand, nervousness about a successful exit stops investors from entering in the first place. It also means there's less capital being recycled for reinvestment.

What do you need to get the money?

People are often surprised when angel funders or venture capitalists don't leap at investing in their great idea. That's not because conditions are tight. Even

TRAGICALLY, HE LACKED FUNDING TO INVENT THE OTHER WHEEL

101

in good times, you can't expect investors to just hand over money to an untested notion.

A start up is a business proposition, not just an idea. You may have a dream, but if that's all it is, it's likely you'll just dream on.

You need to put yourself on the other side of the table. After all, if you are starting up you are going to invest the next couple of years and most of your spare cash in this idea. Investors have a vested interest in this working out, but so do you.

Before you plunge in, give your proposal a reality check from an investor's point of view.

The first hurdle is having a product, not just a concept. A diligent investor wants to see and test a working model. Too often I see a very carefully designed business plan. It underwrites a great PowerPoint presentation but there is no product; not even a prototype or a rough demo model.

Investors want to be able to look at, and feel, something. That includes proposals for service companies. They want to take a thorough walk through the service you are going to offer. When investors can't see a working model of some sort, they know you are going to come back and ask for more money later. You'll need the first tranche to develop the product, and a second one to get it to market. That means there's more risk. The cost of raising the funds will rise as a result.

Secondly, having some barriers to entry will help enormously. First mover advantage is a powerful dynamic but the rapid emergence of look-alike competition can quickly erode even your worst-case revenue forecasts. You need some time inside the city walls.

This is a big problem for technology start-ups. The accessibility of the cloud – pretty much a wall-free entity – means good ideas that are easy to launch can be quickly duplicated and commoditised. Once that happens, profitability gets squeezed.

Deal sites are a classic case. Early movers generated strong subscriber bases and good returns but the business model was under heavy margin pressure within two years.

Thirdly, if you've got something that works, will it work in the market? You may have technical proof-of-concept, but do you have commercial proof? If you can realistically demonstrate demand, you are asking for money to roll it out rather than build it. You have already started to de-risk the investment and it's looking more attractive.

Lastly, if you successfully raise funds, will the business be capable of self-sustaining growth?

The turn-off for early stage investors is not so much having to ante up for a second round of founding. It's the reason for it. It's fine for a marketing rollout. But if it's for more product development rather than revenue generation, investor appetite will be limited.

If there is appetite at all, the cost of raising those funds – in terms of the equity you have to give away, or the caveats they will demand – will be correspondingly higher.

DOES YOUR PROPOSAL HAVE WHAT IT TAKES?

You may have a comprehensive business plan and a great PowerPoint presentation – everyone does – but do you have a working model with clear commercial potential? Will you have some time to build momentum in a walled city? When the drawbridge is finally lowered and the marketplace rushes in, you will need critical mass, market traction and competitive edge. Will you have it?

You can you tick all those boxes and still get it wrong, but there are investors who will take that chance, including you. Before you commit, make sure it's ready. Ships are often launched before they are finished, but they are never launched before they can float.

$$34$$

The Successful Exit

To take more with you, leave more behind

So you've run a good business and you're ready to move on. You might have a succession plan with options for your employees. Possibly you are looking for a trade sale to the highest bidder. If you are big enough, a public listing might be the way out. Maybe you just want to hand it on to your children – usually the lowest bidders.

Whichever route you choose, you will still want the optimal result. How should you approach this?

On an aircraft, they broadcast emergency procedures as you taxi down the runway. The idea is to show you how to exit in the safest manner. It's meant to be the most orderly solution. In any given circumstances, the fewest people will get hurt and the optimum number will survive.

A successful business exit is not a lot different. If you put together the right plan and execute it in an orderly manner, you leave all parties in the best possible shape.

The stress is on "all parties". In the case of the aircraft, not just the pilot or the passenger in the last row of economy. In the case of a business: the employees, the new owners and you. In other words, everyone survives.

Why does that matter?

The answer lies in another question. Who wants to pay a full price to buy a business that won't survive?

It's all very well to exit at the top, but just like stock market timing, that's just luck. Few people get that lucky. People who get stocks right don't take lucky punts; they have an investment strategy they apply over a time.

For a business investment, the same applies: what's your time horizon and what is the exit strategy? You need the time to put your house in order. Whatever strategy you choose – any of the options in the opening paragraph – the business will more than likely have to be valued, whether you sell it, merge it, or, these days, even if you give it away.

The aim of the successful exit, then, is to take action that presents a sale-ready business, which optimises that value.

What optimises value?

Here are four things that should form part of your strategy.

Sustainability: you need to leave a viable business behind. Few people will pay up for something that doesn't have identifiable recurrent income. What's the point of investing in a business with great momentum if it's likely to slow the moment ownership changes? You may have a variety of income streams, but which ones have a strong future? For a successful exit, strengthen your strongest recurrent income. They are the ones that buyers will value the most.

Brand: it's not all about you. Without meaning to bruise your ego, potential buyers will want to know that you are not crucial to the profitable operation of the business. After all, you're leaving.

If you are an owner, the simplest way to insure against its dependence on you is to develop a template for the management of every aspect of the business – from product design, through accounting and operations, and

on to customer service. If all those things are done consistently, you have a brand. People know what they will get when they deal with the business. It doesn't change when you leave. Turn that template into a manual. That's what investors will be buying. It's the same principle as franchising.

Succession: draw up an org chart – first by function, then by name. List all the essential functions that make the business work. Then look at who is going to do what when you are missing. What needs to be in place to ensure the business remains sustainable and true to brand, with or without you?

Potential Leverage: most businesses sell for a multiple of their earnings. Usually it is based on your track record, but that's not the only yardstick. If it is unencumbered, it may be that potential buyers will fund the purchase by gearing it up. That means a higher price.

Similarly, you may not have the financial wherewithal to take your business to the next level. A larger firm may have those resources and they may be willing to pay upfront for the growth they feel they can bring. Can you position your business on the springboard such that the potential is clear to all enquirers?

These principles apply to any firm, whether for sale or not. They create a functional business that has value. They are also the key ingredients behind a sale-ready structure. They are what buyers look for. If you want to take more value with you when you leave, plan to leave a functional business behind.

35

Have you got enough fuel in the tank?

Staying realistic when all those around you are billionaires

One statistic doing the rounds is this: to build an audience of 50 million people, it took radio thirty-eight years; for television, it was thirteen; the internet took four; Facebook was there in six months.

The drama is not so much the audience growth; it's the speed with which new communication channels have become dominated by the few.

The early automobile industry consisted of thousands of producers. It was 50 years before it was down to a dozen or so global players. It was only when the assembly line began to force up capital costs that the number of players started to shrink.

Not so with the Internet. Most of us could set up an online presence in a few hours, probably for free. Yet a handful of large firms already dominate the space.

Facebook. Google. Amazon. When it comes to delivering content, the new elephants are already in your living room.

How did they do it?

Consumer decisions are driven by convenience. That means simplicity: no

confusion, attractive pricing, minimum time. In online speak, the fewest clicks.

I like browsing in bookshops, but I can also download an electronic version of *War and Peace* in about two minutes on my eReader. The last time I looked, the Kindle edition of the complete works of Tolstoy was going for $1.99. And that's the annotated version too. The bookshop alternative doesn't just look less convenient; it suddenly looks expensive.

The new players thrive on low price and easy access. Want to join Facebook? Put in your name and a password and you're on. Want to send a message? Type and press enter. Search on Google? Input your query and go. All free.

We already knew this. It's why there's always a queue at the McDonald's takeout window. If you want to dominate your space, be the most convenient and inexpensive supplier on your block.

But that's not the only thing they did. All three survived on venture capital. Amazon didn't turn profitable until its seventh year – even then only modestly, and after cutting costs, tightening budgets and focusing on profit rather than growth.

It was eight years before Google developed Adwords, which finally moved it into serious profitability. Facebook's audience growth was spectacular but not so its revenues or its share price.

It's one thing to have a big audience. It's another to monetise it. Contrary to popular belief, none of these entities got by on the smell of an oily rag. They rapidly built a pipeline, but it was only when they started putting profitable ideas in the pipe that they could stand alone. Amazon once sold books. Now it sells anything.

In the meantime, it had to survive.

To that extent, starting up is still about cash, whether it's yours or someone else's.

This is the history of most businesses, be they elephants or sole proprietors. The basic rules have not changed with the web. Market share is built on convenience and price but survival is based on cash flow. Businesses don't fail when they don't make a profit. They fail when they run out of money.

Don't let the spectacular statistics blind you to the hard yards. You still have to run a business. It's not a matter of how exciting your idea is. It's a matter of having the resources to survive the start-up grind. To do that – unless you've got some magical business that yields immediate cash flow – you need cash, either yours or, as in the case of these online giants, someone else's.

Make sure you've got access to enough. When you put your business plan together, don't forget the worst-case scenario – the one that assumes that getting there will cost twice as much and take twice as long.

36

The most powerful profit lever

We need to talk about prices

Price is the most powerful profit lever. The arithmetic is simple. If costs are $9 and you sell for $10, your profit margin is 10%. Raise your price 10% to $11 and your profit doubles to $2.

It's also the loss lever. Cut that price by 10% and profit disappears.

Price is the quickest thing you can change in the margin equation. Reducing expenses requires careful planning and execution. Prices can be shifted overnight. Want to move idle stock? Put it on sale.

Price is also the most flexible marketing tool. It can be bundled with other offers. It can make a statement about your quality, attract customers or build loyalty.

Smart pricing is critical to real business success.

Surprisingly few firms align their price with the realities of their market or their business. They opt for the simplest price-setting mechanism: cost plus.

Nothing wrong with that if it works. But business is about optimising returns, not scraping by. Having the right pricing architecture will optimise the value of your business.

This applies to all firms. National suppliers with hundreds of product lines build customer relationships by coupling appropriate pricing with rebates for scale.

At the local coffee shop, a promotion where

customers "get every 10th cup free" applies the same principle. It's an implicit discount for a good customer. Both those firms fiddle with pricing to build business.

HOW TO APPROACH PRICE

Clearly you will want to set prices at a profitable level but you need to think of a range rather than a specific number. Once you've done that, look at the factors that influence each end of the range. Here are some simple guidelines:

- Develop a holistic strategy. Put pricing in a whole-of-firm perspective. What are you trying to achieve in terms of market position and market share? Does your price structure reflect that?
- Focus on value. Examine what problem your product or service solves. What is the value of that solution? How can you improve its appeal or delivery? This is the key to releasing hidden margin and boosting profitability. Small tweaks can make a big difference to the margin equation.
- Be inclusive. Have a pricing team. Get input from others. If you've got the people, ask finance, sales, marketing and operations. You will be surprised at their contribution. You will end up with a more creative policy backed with buy-in and understanding.
- Keep it simple. Build a pricing structure that is easy to comprehend and can be adjusted via simple rules that everyone understands. If you've got a sales team, they need to know their boundaries and where they've got flexibility.
- Investigate alternatives. Look at bundling, selling add-ons, staggered payments, or preferred customer discounts.
- Lastly, don't forget the nature of the actual prices. Something that sells for $4.99 in McDonald's says value. Nothing sells for $34.99 in an upscale restaurant. It'll be on the menu for an even $35 and will scream quality and class. What do your prices say?

Smaller businesses often set prices too low. I have rarely seen anyone lose volume from a 5% increase. This suggests you should review prices at least annually. People expect inflation adjustments. Properly managed, they are an opportunity to boost volume. Market them via special promotions and bundled offers.

Don't hold back from moving prices. Set them at a level that reflects the value you provide. Just make sure you have examined the logic behind it. Make pricing part of a comprehensive strategy that supports your business goals.

37

Failure: do it cheaply and do it less often

Always let the "NO" case be heard

How hard is it to temper enthusiasm? Most business advice these days is about how to rev it up, not tone it down. Try standing up at the end of an inspiring and motivating off-site and suggesting the amazing new strategy might not work.

Not a good look.

There may be good reasons to question the new initiative, but by the time everyone is getting onboard it is probably too late for skepticism to get any traction.

Yet there seems to be no slowdown in business failures, either at the firm level or the product level. In some ways there seems to be more failure. The pace of change puts on pressure for more innovation, not less — and more rapid innovation at that. There's even less time to get it right.

The world is also more complicated. The amount of information and processes out there mean that making mistakes is easier now. There is just too much stuff to take into account. (Seize the day).

So how should we approach failure? It's fashionable to roll out clichés about failure being the way of learning. That's all well and good. We obviously learn from failure. And we need to remember that a single defeat is not a final defeat.

But if failure brings down your business or career in one fell swoop, it's a pretty expensive lesson.

Learning from failure only works if you can identify that you actually have failed. That's not always easy. Few are those who can quickly adjust to getting it wrong. People who make incorrect forecasts and predictions turn first to self-protection: they almost got it right; they would have if only something unexpected hadn't happened; they were wrong for the right reasons; and so on.

Those attitudes get in the way of truly learning from mistakes. You need to fully embrace failure before you can openly and diligently work through a post-mortem.

Doing so is a good process, but can you do something about it earlier? What about a pre-mortem?

INTRODUCE THE NEGATIVE EARLY

Next time you set up a planning weekend or a brainstorming session, set a table aside for the "no" vote. If there is only you, find a devil's advocate.

It is very hard to stress test a "great" idea from the side of enthusiasm. Being positive is an admirable attribute, but if you are focused only on making it work, you may end up making something unworkable.

Give some of your smarter people the task of proving it won't work. Bring in outsiders if you think everyone is just too "onboard" with the idea. See if they can come up with contrary views that simply cannot be ignored.

Build an environment in which people are encouraged to rigorously stress test the proposal and are applauded for their effort. Embrace the uncertainty they create.

Uncertainty can hinder but it can also help. There are three reasons it can have a positive influence:

- It makes it clear that failure is a possibility. Failure is so common we need a mind-set in which it is expected rather than dismissed.
- It will also help you fail cheaply. If the process produces enough evidence to suggest it will be no "sure thing", you are less likely to bet the farm.
- Lastly, it will cultivate broader thinking and open minds. That means the ground might be fertile enough to come up with workable solutions to whatever problems are discovered.

If you are working through an idea or a strategy, raise the negatives early. Who knows, you may come up with a completely different strategy that makes a lot more sense than your original idea. It wouldn't be the first time innovation was triggered by the odd ones out.

Post mortems make sense. By all means have one if your idea doesn't work. But a good pre-mortem could mean you will have fewer of them.

38

Diversity: It's not just about race and gender

What about smart and dumb?

The case for more diversity in management is well-researched. Teams that encourage minority opinions regularly make better decisions than those with a narrow view.

That should be no surprise. Anyone who has stress-tested a "great idea" knows it will be more robust if it's intensely critiqued. While technical ability and relevant knowledge play a big part in effective management, it is openness and enquiry that fine-tune successful decisions.

Business history is littered with corporate failures due to single-minded boards and CEOs. It's the core message behind arguments for countering gender bias or mono-cultural input in senior management.

Nonetheless, it needs to be real. In the same way that corporate social responsibility has little real impact when it is mindlessly bolted onto a mission statement, diversity achieves little unless management draws on all its inherent strengths.

Diversity is not just a populist matter of race or gender. It comes in all shapes and sizes. Take smart people. We all know they are useful. Yet they also represent only one input and they come with their own limitations.

Smartness often involves having a lot of so-called "working memory" – the ability to juggle a lot of information at one time. It gives those people the ability to work with complex issues.

The downside? Studies show that people with a lot of working memory will often opt for the most complicated process or the more complex solution. They can use up all their mental horsepower and fail to spot the optimal answer, which might be something much simpler.

What's the upside for us dumber people? The advent of the MRI has helped neuroscientists make a lot of statistically significant findings in this area. There are too many to cover here, but a short list would include:

- Smarter people find answers to difficult questions more easily when they are working on them with dumber people.
- Smarter people can focus, but it can prevent them from seeing all the alternatives. Dumber people, whose brains don't inhibit the entry of distracting ideas, see them more easily.
- Smart people tend to be more perfectionist and are hard on themselves. That leads to more stress and less efficient decision-making. Dumber people more easily see excuses for their lack of perfection and are less stressed as a result.

Then there is the "cocktail party" effect. People with less working memory inadvertently eavesdrop. They are more likely to hear their name mentioned by others in a crowded room, whereas people with strong working memory concentrate on the conversation they are having.

Most studies describe the cocktail party effect as a bad thing, but frankly, there are times when it is pretty useful, if you don't get so hammered on the cocktails that you misinterpret the information.

Diversity is a spur to innovative thinking. If you are putting together a think tank to generate new ideas, or test them out, don't limit participation to the politically correct categories.

Take advantage of gender and cultural differences but look as well for broader differences in thinking patterns. Smart people will help, but so will dumb ones. It will also improve my chance of getting picked on the team.

39

Growing your business: build it or buy it?

One plus one usually equals one, or less

Of all the great strategic buzzwords, the dubious merit award goes to synergy. Often trotted out as the most remarkable logic behind some of the greatest mergers, its track record is dreadful.

Growth through acquisitions might work for some, but not for most. Even research by consulting heavyweights – that is, the people who often advise on mergers and acquisitions – show that in most cases, it doesn't work. One study by Bain & Co found that fully two-thirds of takeovers reduced the value of the acquiring company.

There are lots of reasons. Cultural fit is one. Instead of embracing change, cultures usually clash. Technology platforms are another. They usually collide rather than collaborate. It's often expensive. Two years after merging in 2000, Time Warner/AOL famously wrote down the value of their synergistically merged entity by $99bn.

That puts a focus on price, which is usually too high. Rupert Murdoch wrote down the Wall St Journal by $2.8bn within two years of

buying it for $5.6bn. Buying ABN Amro pretty well broke the Royal Bank of Scotland overnight. That was a bank that had been travelling reasonably well for about 280 years.

You don't have to be a corporate heavyweight to suffer. The tech wreck was littered with failed mergers and roll-ups of small tech companies. Retail mergers have a particularly spotty history. Even where small partnerships are formed, I rarely find both partners particularly happy with the result.

So if you've got a business, how should you think about buying another one?

Here are a few simple guidelines for getting a realistic perspective.

If you are worried about cultural fit, form an alliance first. It's a way to find out things you won't find out in the due diligence room – including whether your customers think it's a great idea. You'll also get a better view of each other's value and whether or not you can actually work together.

Assume your systems are not compatible. Has anyone ever known an IT project that didn't over-promise and under-deliver? Instead of thinking about the savings from combined platforms, work out what it will cost to integrate them.

If you are buying business lines or sales teams, examine how much it would cost to build them yourself. The history of synergy indicates that for every $1000 you spend, you will get less back. If you are still prepared to spend that $1000, what could you build yourself?

Ditto for buying a business to buy customers. How many do you think the acquisition will yield? How much would it cost you to buy that many customers yourself?

Whatever you do, form a "no" group. M&A is exciting. Task some of your best people to examine why this is not a good idea. The logic behind acquisition is alluring. It includes all those strategic aims of growing capacity, boosting market position, expanding geographically, cross-selling, stronger teams, better distribution, or buying the competition, just to mention a few.

Get your "no" group to critically examine why you can't do all that yourself for the same price. You never know, you might end up with a really sensible business plan – one that leaves your culture intact and grows your business in a way that actually gives you a return on your investment.

You may even end up with a fantastic business that someone wants to acquire for a silly price. There seem to be plenty of them about.

40

Finding better ideas

Evolutions versus revolution

Innovation has been a dominant management buzzword in recent years. Suddenly entire business strategies have been mapped out with this word as the focal point. It makes it sound like innovation is somehow "new" and therefore potentially revolutionary.

In reality what's been happening is more like evolution. It's going on all around you and has been for some time. The more intense focus that "innovation" has prompted calls for some caution. In business, you can spend a lot of time looking for an innovative breakthrough while your competitors are constantly evolving.

Innovation is a lot closer to older terms like "product development". Not quite as exciting, I admit, but that's a similar process that achieves the same outcome: it makes things better and more marketable.

Breakthrough inventions are rare. There are millions of entrepreneurs, but not many inventors. Successful entrepreneurs are the people who make an invention work in the marketplace. Henry Ford did not invent the V8 engine. He saw a market for it and insisted his engineers develop one. That was an innovative process.

Today there is a market for a clean, green engine. There is nothing new about an electric car but the hunt is on for one that is better and more marketable. Slowly – perhaps too slowly for some – such a product will evolve.

Successful innovation is also not always a matter of invention. Touch-screen technology, which enabled Apple to virtually own an entire sector of the PC market, was not invented by Apple. Rather, it was made functional and fashionable by Apple. Innovation doesn't confine itself to physical products. There can be major innovations in marketing, service or distribution channels.

PUTTING A SIMPLE INNOVATION PROCESS IN PLACE

All businesses are surrounded by ideas. Use people both inside and outside your firm to express them. New initiatives come from diverse perspectives – customers, suppliers, operations people, even competitors. If you want some lateral ideas, set up an inclusive think tank and spend an hour examining your existing product from these perspectives:

- Environment: what's changing. Products have life cycles. Where is yours in the cycle? Do you need to adapt your existing product or develop a new one?

- Complexity: think of the opposite version of your product. If your have a premium item, consider a lite one. If it's simple, investigate a complex one that solves more of the customer's problems.

- Value: how elastic is your market? If you want bigger margins, what add-ons would underwrite higher prices in profitable volume?

• Range: unbundle your offerings into more marketable parcels. Develop new versions or upgrades. Build a developmental sequence into your range.

• Collaboration: if you don't have the product in your range, form an alliance with someone who does.

• Lateral: you've got a customer base. What else do they spend money on? Introduce adjacent products that capture a bigger share of their wallet.

This doesn't only work for physical products. Services develop in the same way. Look at the emergence of premium movie theatres. They acknowledge that the environment now includes a demographic that wants a premium offering.

These theatres provide a more complicated product in a bundled form that offers higher value, capturing a bigger share of the consumer's wallet. Instead of going to a bar for drinks, followed by a restaurant for dinner and then a movie, premium theatres do the lot in one venue, leveraging off the same film they are already showing in standard theatres.

Brainstorm some fresh ideas around these themes. An hour spent on this process may not immediately lead to a major new innovation, but it will show you where to start looking. Make a habit of it and you will start to build innovative momentum.

41

The sustainable opportunity

Aligning your business with the planet

The profit motive is not flavour of the decade. It's blamed for a lot of things, not least environmental degradation and global warming. Yet it is the profit motive that ensures a business does not fail, that it continues to make things people want and that people are employed doing so.

Business should be rightly worried about this inherent conflict. Public concern about the environment is growing, not receding. Business can resist the trend, but it is a market reality. What happens if we embrace it?

The word sustainability has been around for a while. It may have been hijacked by the climate change debate, but it dates back to the 13th century and derives from the French word *sustenir*, meaning to endure.

Does anyone not want their business to endure?

For many, the response is to appear "green", to make cosmetic changes in the hope of attracting environmentally conscious consumers. It often works but soon everyone else is doing it.

Efforts at the strategic level can be equally vacuous. You can bolt sustainability onto your values statement, but how will that help your business endure? It won't do much for you – or the planet – unless it translates into action.

There is a sounder alternative. One that is more thorough and makes more business sense. That is to align sustainability with your profit motive; to use the notion to explore product and

process innovation that help your business endure, along with the environment.

An example is logistics firm, UPS, which set up a team to examine sustainable initiatives. One was redesigning its delivery routes. This resulted in some extremely simple ideas; like eliminating left hand turns so vehicles no longer idled away waiting for a gap in the traffic or a change of lights. The result? For the planet, a saving of around 20,000 metric tones of CO_2 emissions; for UPS, a significant cut in the fuel bill.

This is a real contribution to the sustainability of both. It's given the firm competitive edge through lower costs in a way that achieves a social outcome. It's a sustainable initiative that is now embedded in the business model.

Management academic, Michael Porter, made this same point in a landmark piece in Harvard Business Review. He called it "shared value", which, contrary to Corporate Social Responsibility (CSR) or philanthropy, is "self-interested behavior that creates economic value by creating social value".

As tough economic conditions have put philanthropic funding under pressure, the concept of social investment bonds has emerged. They are based on the same principle. They look to invest in programs that deliver outcomes, which, in the long term, become self-sustaining and ultimately lead to savings for the government or the philanthropic provider.

SO WHERE DOES YOUR SELF-INTERESTED BEHAVIOR COME IN?

Try using sustainability as a focus for profitable innovation. You won't be solving global warming today, but run a checklist over your operations and ask some simple questions.

Inputs: you don't have to be UPS. For my equine business, it's using grey water for irrigation, solar for power and recycled horse manure for fertiliser. All three lower costs and produce a better result for everyone, including the horses. British Sugar redirected waste hot water and CO_2 to massive glasshouses where it grows tomatoes. Doing so lifted their tomato production by more than 40%. What are you doing with your waste?

Products: United Biscuits cut its material needs by 16% by using recyclable lightweight packaging, reducing its transport charges as well. Making anything lighter usually lightens costs.

People: wellness programs for employees reduce absenteeism, cut staff turnover and reduce health costs. Porter quotes Johnson and Johnson as saving $2.17 for every $1 spent on wellness programs. In a country known for the high cost of employee health care, that amounted to $250m over 5 years.

Market: your customers may demand this. Consumers increasingly favour organic food, recycled packaging and products with a low carbon imprint. Prices on those goods are often higher, but so are margins.

Growth: Australian bank, ANZ, targeted Asian growth. Applying its existing technology to an underdeveloped market, it launched a branchless banking system in Cambodia offering retail banking and payment services over mobile phones. Called Wing, it captured 20% of the bank account market in less than two years.

Supply chains: more corporations ask suppliers for their green credentials. If you want to remain a preferred supplier, you may have no choice. The challenge is to meet their demands and improve your profitability at the same time.

Environmental sustainability and the profit motive often appear conflicted but they don't necessarily have to oppose each other. What can you do to bring them into alignment? A more creative – and enduring – accommodation is one that embraces the notion of sustainability rather than resists it.

42

Staying bootstrapped

Using frugal strategies

Want to reinvent your business? One strategy is to return to the startup model. It reinvigorates the enthusiasm and drive that characterise a business launch, spurring innovation and idea generation.

We see it in notions like "skunkworks" and "idea labs". These are initiatives that try to remove the innovative process from the strictures of existing operations and procedures. Set up in an open and unfettered environment, they are designed to encourage new thinking, and with it, new, workable ideas.

The track record, however, is patchy. Ideas emerge, but they often lack traction in the marketplace. Plenty of great innovations are stillborn; they are long on vision but lack financial discipline.

What's missing? A key business instinct behind successful startups is survival. They rarely begin with fountains in the lobby and nicely laid out open plan offices. That can all come later. The more likely launching pad is the garage.

Short of funds, the startup has to make it work on a limited budget. New businesses have to focus on cash flow in order to survive. That can generate innovations that are just as important as the "great idea".

Harvard professor, Ian Macmillan, called this a strategy of asset parsimony. It is based on the idea of doing as much as possible with as little as possible. The definition of parsimony is an extreme unwillingness to spend money or use resources.

Some of Macmillan's guidelines:

> Do not buy new what you can buy second-hand.
>
> Do not buy what you can lease.
>
> Do not lease what you can barter.
>
> Do not barter what you can borrow.
>
> Do not borrow what you can salvage.
>
> Do not salvage what you can get for free.

Not a bad list. You can use it to review any business project – new or old.

Applying parsimony is a matter of asking what can you actually achieve with the amount you have, or finding ways of raising more within your existing modus operandi.

- For example, positive cash flow comes from getting more money in. But it also comes from reducing the amount going out. Revenue-producing initiatives are innovative, but so are expense-saving ideas.

- Maybe you need to streamline your ambition. What is the simplest route to get to the first goal? What 20 per cent of the effort gives the most result? This is necessarily more productive than the other 80%.

- Investigate free resources and less-expensive alternatives. Need a vehicle? A new one will lose 25% of its value the moment you drive out of the dealership. Buy second-hand – and lease it.

- Look on the net for resources at steep discounts. Anybody can now make a first-phase website in a few hours using free software. Cut communication costs with Skype. You don't need an office if a virtual one will do. What resources do friends and colleagues have? Can you collaborate to the benefit of both parties?

- Firms are slow to liquidate assets that take up valuable space and require maintenance. Do you have assets that can be rented out during their downtime? What can you sell on eBay?

When the Apollo 13 moon mission appeared doomed, engineers on the ground physically collected samples of the resources available on the spacecraft: plastic tubing, bits of wire, odd electronic parts. Working through the night they crafted a jury-rigged solution. The astronauts repeated it in space. It was enough to save the mission.

Whether you are reinventing your business or starting a new one, try applying parsimony to reinvigorate financial discipline. It is easier to find alternative cheaper solutions when the expensive ones aren't around. The chances of new ideas being financially successful will improve as a result.

43

What's your best opportunity?

Simple rules about creating value

I once addressed a group of CEOs all of whom had a common problem. The workshop was held in an Asian city. At the time, the region was on a roll. As a result, all of their businesses were cash flow positive. They had it coming in quicker than it was going out. Funds were piling up in the bank.

So what's the problem?

Clearly they had no pressing issues. Survival wasn't a concern. Nor was growth. What they were mostly concerned about was optimising the value of their business.

The fact is, money in the bank earns well below the return on capital they usually generate in their business. The excess cash wasn't really creating value.

It's the opposite of leverage. If you borrow money for less than the return you generate on that money, you create value. In theory at least.

The mirror image is net cash. If your firm is returning 10% on the capital it uses but your cash on deposit gets only 5%, it drags down the overall return on capital employed by your business.

Not a bad problem to have, but the mathematics of it mean the value of your business is diminished.

Can you do anything about it?

Should you do anything about it? There is nothing wrong with a bit of cash in the buffer. Its one reason my audience were prosperous survivors.

At the same time, there may be

IT'S A POSTMODERN PROFIT, RUNNING AT A LOSS

opportunities going past the window. What's a framework for making investment decisions in this environment?

There may be no immediate risk, but the rules of risk management can help. They don't only apply when things are going wrong. They also make sense when things are going right.

The first is "don't bet the farm". So work out just how big a buffer you want. After that, what are some rules you can apply when deciding if it's worth betting a bit of the farm? Here are four of them.

- Do what you know. Look close to home. That's where you know what you are doing. Can you buy into customers or suppliers? If you have market strength in delivering your product, is there an adjacent product you can put in the pipe? If you rent your premises, should you buy them?
- Identify negative triggers. What could go wrong? Don't stop at the immediate impact of a disastrous event. Expect contagion. What are the knock-on effects? How exposed will you be if an unexpected Black Swan sails in?
- Impact. If it does go wrong, how bad will it be? If the return is right, it may be worth the risk. Just be clear what the risk is. Which brings us to;
- Probability. How likely is the disastrous scenario? Ultimately, that will decide the risk you are taking and what the return should be. Put it in percentage terms. It needs be comfortably ahead of deposit rates.

Risk management doesn't eliminate disaster, but it puts a framework around your decision. It reduces the chance of destroying more value than your surplus cash is destroying while it sits on deposit.

If you can't find an investment that jumps over the risk bar, there is always an alternative. It's called a dividend.

44

The power of doubt

To make better decisions, embrace uncertainty

In the 1990s, I was running a trading team in New York. When staff and clients arrived at our annual Christmas party, we would ask them to name one stock that would beat the market in the next year.

This was important information. After all, we are talking about highly educated fund managers and savvy traders, the smartest people in the room.

We also had a dartboard. We would plaster it with the share price lists from the *Wall St Journal*. Then we'd get everyone to throw a dart. We'd keep a record of that too.

I can't remember a year when the dartboard wasn't the overall winner.

Expert frailty is now widely acknowledged.

Today we can be fairly certain that smart people are often wrong, especially when predicting.

This plays out in the investment world. Last year's best performing investment fund is almost certain not to be the best in the coming year. It's also a certainty that significantly more funds will underperform the market than outperform it.

When you think about it, that makes sense. It's mathematically impossible for everyone to outperform the market.

We can perhaps forgive ourselves for lousy

OPTION *B

forecasts if they are about things of which we know little. But we need to remember that educated experts don't generally predict well either. Often a shot in the dark is nearer the mark.

In one MIT project, a group given only minimal market information invested far more successfully than those exposed to the full gamut of investment news and advice.

A 2005 Princeton study found the predictions of political pundits to be incorrect almost 70% of the time.

Is there a common thread amongst those getting it wrong?

Empirical evidence suggests predictive failure is more likely to occur amongst those who are "certain" they are right.

Research results show this to be the case regardless of the skill-set or the political persuasion of the expert. Fundamental investment analysts fail as often as technical analysts. Left leaning commentators and right wing forecasters are equally hopeless.

The only thing they seem to have in common is the certainty they have of their own view.

And here's another worrying fact. Guess which gender research shows to be the most certain they are right. Yes, you guessed it. Men. A landmark analysis of 35,000 investors published in MIT's Quarterly Journal of Economics showed male investors to be significantly overconfident, trade more on the back of that confidence and to underperform female investors as a result.

Men are the people who largely managed the financial sector right through the global financial disaster. And by and large, they are still in charge. Scary isn't it? And I'm a man.

So we need to be wary of those who sound certain. And not just men.

Before I'm accused of gender bias I should mention that one of the most compelling analysts I know is a woman. She always

touches my nervous buttons. She can articulate the downside of any situation with engaging grace and elegance. If I stuck to her advice, I would have missed every bull market in history.

All this supports the call for greater diversity. It's not a matter of political correctness. It's the need for better decision-making. Nor is it confined to the financial sector. The business environment is not just more complicated. It's also more complex. Managing complexity requires diverse input.

For complicated systems, there is usually a road map. The manufacturing assembly line was complicated but if you followed the manual you could manage the process. Complexity is another matter. It's about the growing inter-connectedness of the supply chain.

It looks simple but it's complex.

A virtual business is a good example. You can start an online shopping mall tonight. Click and drag a selected manufacturer's range over to your site. Bolt on a shopping cart and a payment system. Start taking orders and transmit them to the manufacturer. They deliver them to the customer's door.

This is a hands-free business. You don't touch the stock or meet the customer. There's no warehousing. You don't package the product or deliver it. Just collect the money up front, pay the manufacturer's invoice and keep your commission.

But you are no longer in charge. Anything could go wrong and you wouldn't know it. Even then, you probably couldn't do much about it. Group buying sites are already finding this to their cost.

Inter-connectedness is a feature of modern business, be it a virtual mall or a global corporation. A failure in one area leads to knock-on effects that could not have been easily predicted.

In the financial crisis, business laid off risk in derivative markets. It made a lot of sense until those markets failed. The complex nature of derivative products meant the problem was contagious. Failure went viral.

Mixed input increases the chance of getting it right. If you want to stress-test an idea, you are unlikely to get a great result if everyone in the room has the same perspective.

This means including people other than the smartest ones. Research suggests smart people make better decisions when they work with not-so-smart people. Mixed-ability teams regularly outdo all-star teams. They generate more ideas and come up with simpler solutions which are easier to implement.

There are no right or wrong ways to accommodate this, but here are a few suggestions:

- Look for diverse input. Spend some time brainstorming why the great idea won't work. You may uncover some issues, but also ways to solve them.
- Examine why the dartboard can win. This will introduce real lateral thinking into your decision-making. It may even give you a better idea.
- Check your intuition. Acknowledge your own experience. It sends emotional signals to you, both positive and negative. Don't depend on them, but listen to them all the same. How does the idea feel? Why?

No matter how good your plan is, things can shift rapidly in a complex environment and often in surprising areas. Relying on a single strategy becomes problematic when the situation changes. To counter inert decision making, embrace uncertainty. Be aware of alternatives. Use the solvent of doubt to adjust your strategy to fit the situation.

45

The Entrepreneur's Dream

Kodak moment for mobile apps

Instagram. It's a story for these times. Young geek collaborates with Silicon Valley network to build simple but popular product. Engages customers with social media to get rapid market traction. Risk-taking venture capitalists provide cash while user base grows to 30 million. Within two years, with a total staff of 13 and zero revenues, the business is sold to Facebook for a billion dollars.

To put the story in stark relief with the old economy, that's more than the value of *The New York Times*, a newspaper that has been around since 1851. It's also more than the closing market value of fading photographic giant, Eastman Kodak.

What's changed here?

Mobile technology for one. This is the power of the mobile app writ large. On one hand, Instagram is just a photo-sharing network. On the other, you can photograph anything, anytime, and send it to anyone, anywhere, in just a few seconds, for free. You can fiddle with the photograph and interface with your social media. It's a personal tool but the business prospects for this kind of simplicity are staggering.

Speed. The whole process is faster, not just the product but also time to market. From concept to launch was barely six months. Early

adopters loved it. Social media marketing generated 25,000 users in the first 24 hours. The ability to disrupt, and to gather rapid traction, is more and more a function of how quickly you can shift from idea to market.

Design. In this market it can trump function. There are similar products but this one looks good. Even the icon for the app is cuter than most others. Founders Kevin Systrom and Mike Krieger ensured the look and feel matched the hype.

What hasn't changed?

Cash flow. The numbers sound small now but initial injections of $250,000 by friends and angel investors kept the project ticking over. Unlike a lot of good ideas, it didn't run out of money before getting traction.

Collaboration. Systrom didn't do it alone. He drew extensively on his Stanford alumni. Krieger was a member of an entrepreneurial development group to which they both belonged. Skills and venture capital came directly from their networking activities.

Customers. That's what drove the value. It's hard to price a business with no revenue. The deal was equal to just over $30 per user. In terms of buying customers, that's not cheap, but it's in the ballpark for social app values. Presumably Facebook thinks it can generate value per user which is in excess of this number. As a measure of market penetration, customers still matter. Sometimes it's cheaper to buy them than build them.

Market power. The real value of a niche strategy comes from dominating your niche. Facebook paid a premium for that strength. The transaction not only took out a potential rival, it kept it out of the hands of the other big elephants in the social media room. Market power is still what makes you strategically attractive.

Did they just get lucky?

Maybe, but those are the things that made that luck. In the opposite of a perfect storm, everything went right. Even the rich buyer turned up.

They are also the things that grow the worth of any business. The playing field may be changing, but value is still generated by maintaining good cash flow, leveraging ideas by collaborating with others and putting customers first. They build the market power that other people want to buy. Keep them well-oiled.

46

Stay ahead by doing more of the same

Does rapid change calls for big shifts in strategy?

It's all going quicker. Product cycles are shorter. So is time to market. And, so the logic goes, marketing strategies and selling propositions need to change as well. Is that right?

On the contrary, refocusing on your core message can guide you through the complexity and overthinking that often characterises rapid change. It keeps the business grounded and the firm's identity intact.

CUSTOMERS STILL WANT THE SAME THING

When touch screen technology arrived, No one asked how it worked. They just started using it because it was easy. You don't have to explain a complex product development to the market. It doesn't want to know. The market embraced touch screens because they were simple to use. It's not as if you needed training.

If your core message is quality and you deliver an advanced version through a more complex process, your task is still to deliver quality. Rolex has either led or adopted every advance in watchmaking technology, but it's still a Rolex. That's why people buy them. It's a quality brand.

The key to monetising product development is improving your product without losing sight of your key message. That's what already differentiates you from the competition. What you need to do is enhance the power of your difference.

Say it's convenience. Is your advanced version or new range still more convenient to buy or easier to use than an alternative? The market will appreciate the innovation and improvement but, crucially, your key point of differentiation has again asserted itself in the market. They can depend on you to be convenient.

Ditto for any core message, whether it's speed of delivery, consistency of brand, scalability, or design. If that is what people love about your product or service, drive it even harder when you make an innovation. Drive you new initiatives in that direction.

Say it's customer service. That's something that can generate as much sales growth as technology. I go to the Apple store because smart young people half my age almost fall over themselves to help me solve a relationship issue between my iPad and my iPhone. And that's *after* I've bought a product, not when they are trying to talk me into it. It's not surprising that I'll likely buy another.

Key messages don't change when other things do. Successful innovation is doing better what you already do best.

Maintaining that mantra is an inside job. For it to work, you need to embrace it internally.

Service is a great example. How often do people think that providing "great service" only applies to counter staff?

Clearly those customer-facing people are a key part of your market interaction, but what are the people in the back office doing to help staff provide that great service?

Ask other questions that push the same button. Is the driver behind new innovations delivering even greater service? Does management walk the walk by serving their staff? Do procurement officers look to how they can serve the suppliers who in turn are serving them?

If everyone in the firm is serving each other you will have the sort of culture that ensures the customer gets optimum service.

As a powerful differentiator, your key message needs to infiltrate the entire eco-system of the business. If everyone is on the same page, all decisions become simpler and they all work toward maintaining your competitive edge.

It's simple propositions that drive market presence. They don't change when the product does. They just become more important and more powerful.

47

The Collaborative Cockpit

Good managers are neither ideologues nor cynics

Before the acronym CRM was hijacked by Customer Relationship Management, it stood for Cockpit Resource Management. Developed by NASA in the 1970s, it was a collaborative practice aimed at curbing disasters due to human error.

This original CRM was later adopted by commercial airlines. It is still a key part of aircrew training. It's credited with a two-decade fall in the number of aircraft mishaps caused by people rather than malfunction.

What are the main tenets? They are things that easily translate to business practices. Eschew certainty. Be aware that unexpected developments are exactly that: unexpected. Encourage debate. Use all available resources. Understand that you may be wrong. Pilots themselves need to be open to question.

Putting all that into practice means not restricting the source of information to hard assets like data, or on an aircraft, instrumentation. The former can create a false image; the latter can fail. Equally, the people in charge, like airline captains, need to allow doubters a voice.

Take this incident. In 1989, prior to crashing on takeoff in Ontario, Canada, passengers alerted a DC9 cabin crew to massive icing on the plane's wings. The

stewardess, however, felt too intimidated by crew hierarchy to pass the information onto the flight deck. The result? 42 dead.

The implications for managing anything are obvious. Get more input and get it from a wider variety of sources.

Right now – and maybe never – no single ideology has the answers. Yet we seem more and more extreme in our views rather than accepting alternative explanations.

Communism may have failed but last time I checked, capitalism hadn't hit any home runs recently either. Antidotes to current crises are equally split. Half the world thinks the solution to Europe's woes is austerity. The other half say it's growth.

It's likely somewhere in between. Despite the attraction of black or white explanations, reality is generally grey.

So too for management theory.

The latest fads are often just that and usually address only an element of the business equation. Many have little traction in the broader workplace.

Leadership training, currently in vogue, focuses on senior management rather than encouraging everyone to lead at their own level. In the words of Harvard professor, Henry Mintzberg: "we are over-led and under-managed."

What's happening with the flight attendants in your business?

The success of CRM suggest the likelihood of wrong decisions is reduced by facilitating debate and encouraging people at all levels to express their opinions.

The manager's role?

Be an informed skeptic. Avoid the closed mind of the cynic and be open to lateral ideas regardless of their source. Cynics reject novel opinions outright; skeptics ask to be convinced. Give people airtime.

Question the predictions of experts. Stress-test them with scenarios of both success and failure. What if they're wrong?

Allow yourself to be questioned. Value scrutiny of your own decisions.

Most of all, minimise ideology, be it the political variety or management theory. Take what works and leave the rest. The original CRM is just part of pilot training, not all of it.

48

Shareholder value has nothing to do with the share market

Why a lot of executive packages are stupid and outrageous

The level of executive compensation is a perennial source of discontent but despite the noise little is done about it. That's partly because such packages are at their highest in good times. Serious analysis of negative issues gets little traction in good times when everything seems to be ticking over nicely.

One problem is that compensation is often tied to stock prices, which is pretty stupid given that executives are largely powerless over the level of the stock market.

There are two key issues. One is that it forces managers to make tactical moves aimed at boosting their share price in the short term rather than executing a strategy that builds a stronger business over time. Some shareholders might like to see a short-term blip in the price but most want to see sound value being developed in the long run.

THE SOUTH SEA BUBBLE IS BORN

Secondly, it means the rewards that executives get for their effort don't really reflect their effort. It can work against them as much as for them. Take the following example.

A loyal executive of 20 years reaches the rank of CFO. He's smart, thorough and committed. He does a great job, earning options that convert at $10 a share. No one begrudges his package. He's put in the yards and delivered the results.

The share price rises to $15. He plans to retire at 65, exercising his options and using the profit of $5 per share to finance his remaining years.

Next, stock markets tank. The price falls to $5, his options expire worthless and after 20 years contributing to shareholder value, he retires with zip.

His replacement gets the same package. The exercise price is reset to current market at $5; they vest in two years. He's less effective but markets recover. The share price rises to $10. He converts, liquidates and walks, taking with him the value his predecessor had left behind.

Both illustrations are real life examples from the last five years. The compensation of both was tied to increases in shareholder value via the stock market. Did the policy work?

CREATING SHAREHOLDER VALUE VS. TIMING AND LUCK

Four things determine share prices. Management performance can impact on three: earnings, cash flow and dividends. If there is more than one shareholder, the benchmark is how much of those things can be attributed per share. In short, the acronyms common to most investment research EPS, CFPS and DPS.

If you chart the performance of those things, they form a mean to which the share price invariably reverts over time. If they are

STAVROS HAS A BAD DAY.
KNOCKS $3.50 OFF BHP.

strong, so is the share price, relative to market, over time. Vice versa if they are weak.

The most important driver, however, is the state of the market, not the state of the shares. Management has no control over this. In recent years, it's been decided by anything from Lehmann Brothers risk management to Icelandic banks. Lately, Greek voters have been in the driver's seat.

Basing compensation or appraisal on share prices is ridiculous. It's out of management's hands. The argument for it is to align managers' interests with those of shareholders; yet doing so is like expecting your C suite to solve the Euro crisis.

Management needs to have a chance. To encourage that, it needs to be focused on the things that matter. If you are a manager, focus yourself and your team on real increases in shareholder value over time – the extent to which they optimise cash flow and boost earnings per share. These are what determine the ability to pay real things like dividends in real money and lift your rating over time.

If you get that right, you create value. The worth of your business – quoted or not – will increase relative to the marketplace. It will make a private company command a higher sales price and a quoted one a higher share price, relative to where the market is at any time.

As to where the market is at any time, that's a gamble, a matter of timing and luck. It's not something management can do anything about. Shareholder value, on the other hand, is their primary responsibility. Their job is to optimise that value regardless of prevailing conditions. A market is where you realise value, not where you create it.

49

The problem with values

Are lofty statements any use?

Here's a quote: *"Good corporate governance practice is an important ingredient in creating and sustaining shareholder value, and ensuring that behavior is ethical, legal and transparent."*

Nothing special there. Much the same turns up in most value statements. Roughly translated, it says "lets make our business succeed rather than fail, and let's do that by playing fair".

Most people would agree. In fact, to not agree would probably be deemed sociopathic. Values like these are the basis of civilised society and commonly regarded as "normal" behaviour.

So much so, that many of us are suspicious when people insist on stating these things in lofty terms and enshrining them in fancy bold type. It's like saying maybe we are not really like that but we'd like to be.

In the case of this particular quote, that turns out to be the case. It comes from the Barclays Bank website. It's attributed to Chairman of the board.

In 2012, the bank was fined almost half a billion dollars for manipulating market interest rates to it's own advantage. As markets are generally a zero sum game, that means to someone else's disadvantage – in this case, clients, customers and counter parties.

The practice is not what you'd call "fair". It's definitely not ethical. A court of law would probably consider it illegal because they didn't tell anyone. So much for transparency. And as for "creating and sustaining shareholder value" a half a billion fine doesn't help.

Barclay's manipulated LIBOR. That's virtually the official benchmark for huge numbers of financial products. If you have a big trading position in one of them, a fudge of a few basis points can turn a dodgy decision into a million dollar win – something not lost on bonus-conscious traders.

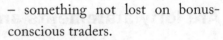

Do values really need to be stated?

Think of someone you respect. Do they stand up and say "Hey, I'm really ethical." Unlikely. The people – and institutions – you respect and trust are the ones who act that way.

How do you honour this in the breach? Rigorous honesty is not always humanity's default position. This is not a Barclay's problem. Nor is it confined to banks. Business is riddled with conflicts between thought and action. So is daily life.

The place to build values is at the coalface – how you treat your colleagues, your customers and your community.

It's not that hard. You don't need to reflect on grandiosity or make pompous statements. Just look at your behaviour: "Is it fair?" It doesn't mean you are not tough, focused or hardworking. It just means you can be trusted. It puts a reliable consistency underneath the way you go about things.

If everyone in your organisation does this, it seeps into the essence of your

HE WHO TAKES THE LAST BISCUIT, WINS

business. It means your colleagues and employees feel safe and appreciated. That culture in turn attracts customer loyalty and eventually manifests in shareholder value.

Trust is a big word, but it is built by small actions that build values over time. They are an outcome of behaviour, not a starting point.

Here's another quote. Dan Ariely, in his excellent book on the trouble with staying honest, puts it very succinctly: *"a small, triggering nudge at the moment of temptation… is more effective than an epic sermon meant to permanently transform your soul."*

50

Beer Mat Strategy

A few ideas can be better than a lot

What was Steve Jobs' first strategic call when he returned to Apple in 1997? According to biographer, Walter Isaacson, Jobs brought back simplicity. After sitting through a review of current projects, he stood before a whiteboard and announced the firm would slash 90% of existing product development.

On the whiteboard he drew a simple alternative plan.

It was a two-by-two matrix. The columns were Consumer and Pro; the rows were Desktop and Portable. Four market segments; four products. Everything else was eliminated. Apple was reborn. We have all watched what has happened since then.

Clear and simple product architecture does not signal a lack of strategic sophistication. Rather, it can cut excessive over think and generate clear focus. Someone like Jobs could use his drive and passion to turn that clarity into an incredibly successful business strategy.

Most of us, however, are not Steve Jobs. We are different people. We have different strengths and we work in different industries. We can learn from him, but we cannot be him. What can we do about this?

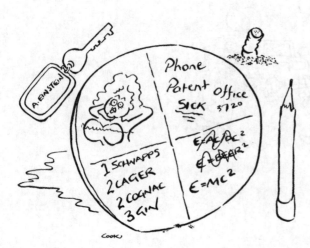

PROMPTING CREATIVE ACTION

Most people do not do their best thinking at work. Good ideas are more likely to come in the shower, or on a walk – times when the mind is not so cluttered. At work there is often just too much going on.

I have seen plenty of great strategies worked out on beer mats or table napkins. Their strength is their clarity, like the mix of simplicity and scribbling that made Steve Jobs' matrix a template for product development.

Try it yourself. Instead of waiting for a major review, assess your business or project now from some very simple perspectives.

Not producing enough profit? Try looking at the profitability of your individual products or customers. It's never even. If you have a range of both, some will contribute handsomely to profit margin; others won't. Some may be a net cost.

Are you focusing your efforts on the most profitable product? For a reality check, plot them on a simple matrix. Mark the top most profitable; the bottom least profitable. On the right hand side, put high volume; on the left, low volume. Then map your product range.

Do you allocate the greatest amount of resources – finance, people, and inputs – to the products in the top right quadrant? Maybe you've got it right, but stand back and look at it. Does it need a rethink, or just a tweak?

What about customers?

Your top customer is not always your best customer. By the time you've adjusted for the cost of servicing them, or the extent to which you finance their payment terms, margins can get pretty thin.

That's before you account for the compensation of the top sales team selling to them or the special services you provide to keep their business.

Is there more margin headroom in selling to other customers? Should you be putting more resources behind servicing them rather than your biggest or dominant customer? Can you also make them "best" customers?

Easiest of all, try 80:20. Put "Effort" on one axis and "Impact" on the other.

What's in the quadrant that produces 80% impact for 20% effort? It's not just a useful business exercise. Try it on your life.

Matrices come in different shapes and sizes, but they all have the advantage of highlighting different perspectives. The ideas of some of the most influential management thinkers – from Michael Porter to Stephen Covey – can be summarised in four quadrants. It's a simple tool; one which didn't do Apple any harm.

NAPOLEON QUICKLY SKETCHED AN INVASION OF RUSSIA

Alan Hargreaves

Alan Hargreaves specialises in simplifying complex business problems. Originally a financial journalist and broadcaster, he spent 35 years in financial services and business consulting. His approach to management is highly effective, yet inspiringly simple. It focuses on real issues rather than strategic principles. His innovative mix of personal and collaborative action brings immediate traction.

Alan is author of the management book, *Recharge*, published by John Wiley and Sons. He is an economics graduate from the University of Sydney. He worked for 20 years in international finance and has built businesses in Hong Kong, Singapore and New York.

Since returning to Australia, he has managed his own private investment trust. Alan has excellent presentation skills and has worked extensively with business audiences through both radio and television. His private equity and advisory services span IT, media, property, finance, communications and retail.

Alan is regularly engaged as a speaker, consultant and mentor. His passions are business, boats and breeding horses.

Patrick Cook

Iconic Australian cartoonist, Patrick Cook, is best known for his weekly commentary in the news magazine, *The Bulletin*, and more recently for his satirical essays and cartoons in the Australian edition of the *The Spectator*.

Patrick's style has had a huge influence on many Australian artists. A Cook cartoon is immediately recognisable. The style is both minimalist and organic, the humour quirky. The subject matter can range from his homicidal wine-swilling koalas to overwrought politicians and social climbers.

Books by Patrick include *Hot and Wet*, *Ship of Fools* and *The Great Big Cook Book*.

Cook's satire considers nothing to be sacred. Unlike many others of his generation, he avoids an obvious political agenda, making his work consistently unpredictable.

Starting in 2011, Patrick collaborated with business writer, Alan Hargreaves, to produce the mix of business humour and insight that characterises their weekly blog, *Recharge*.

We hope you have enjoyed *60 Second Recharge*, the words and insight of Alan Hargreaves with the images and humour of Patrick Cook. Pass it on to friends and associates, revisit and annotate. If you would like to receive the *60 Second Recharge* update just let us know at – *www.wilkinsonpublishing.com.au*

Michael Wilkinson,
Wilkinson Publishing
Great Books From The People You Can Trust